Fans

Hélène Alexander

The Costume Accessories Series
General Editor: Dr Aileen Ribeiro

B.T. BATSFORD LTD
LONDON

In memory of Papa and Mama

ISBN 0 7134 4276 X

Typeset by Tek-Art Ltd, Kent
Printed in Great Britain by
R.J. Acford, Chichester
for the publishers
B.T. Batsford Ltd
4 Fitzhardinge Street
London W1H 0AH

Contents

Acknowledgment

Special thanks go to my friend and wise adviser Madeleine Ginsburg of the Victoria and Albert Museum. I would like to thank my husband, A.V. Alexander, and my daughter Susannah, who kept matters in perspective by their systematic non-co-operation. I am grateful to the following, for their invaluable assistance which has made this book possible: Tom Baker Photographs, Inverness; Anne-Marie Benson, Phillips; Penelope Byrde, Costume Research Centre, Bath; Pat Clegg, Director of Technical Services, Harrogate; Heidi Collins; Aldo Dente; Fabienne Falluel, Musée de la Mode et du Costume, Paris; Colette Hawes; Mr and Mrs Gorand-Hurtes; R. Griffin, National Trust, Waddesdon Manor; Max Harari, Wildenstein, London; Avril Hart, Victoria and Albert Museum; Judy Ingram; J. Ilott, Lewisham Library; Margaret Lyons; Michel Maignan, Duvelleroy, Paris; Joanna Marschner, Court Dress Collection, Kensington Palace; Suzy Mayor, Christies; Mrs McKinlay, Castle Museum, York; Alison Packer, Brighton Museum and Art Gallery; Jeremy Pearson, Royal Albert Memorial Museum, Exeter; F. Perkins Esq., CBE, DSC; Photomus (the John Freeman Group); Vivian Redman; Maria Sepulveda; Fabienne Strum, Musée de l'Horlogerie, Geneva; Kay Staniland, Museum of London; Lorraine Tarran.

All the information on the Maison Duvelleroy in Chapter 5 is recorded by kind permission of the owner, who put the whole archive at my disposal.

List of Illustrations

Introduction

Unlike other accessories to dress, fans can hardly be considered a necessity, especially in the Northern hemisphere. However, it will be seen that, during at least three centuries, fans were as much an adjunct to a lady of fashion's attire as were gloves or bags.

Fans being an established fashion accessory, it is undeniable that they serve a variety of purposes in this capacity. Not only are they a means to cool the brow gracefully with an instrument which is a complement to the dress, but they are also, at the same time, devices which compliment the wearer. Flirting with a fan, 'making eyes' over the top of a decorative object, promises untold delights, just as the correct amount of décolletage is more sensuous than a full display of physical attractions.

Fans were also, throughout their history, a means of disseminating news or political propaganda and as such, whether in the form of a caricature or an advertisement, they are a comment on the social scene of the day.

Within the context of dress, fans assume a considerable importance, although some quite unsubstantiated theories have been put forward in this connection, with no factual evidence to back them up. For example, it is alleged that, in the eighteenth century, the size and span of a fan were in direct proportion with the width and level of the fashionable skirt. This is pure fiction, and there is ample pictorial proof to show a considerable variety of size of fans worn at any one time. (Besides, for sentimental reasons, a woman might be proud to use a fan which was a family heirloom.) It is therefore of special importance to study carefully a wide spectrum of visual documents, such as fashion plates, book illustrations, prints and paintings of everyday life, as well as portraits and set genre pieces. And it is worth remembering that the older woman was more likely to wear an accessory which had been fashionable in her own heyday.

Conversely, it is useful to observe the minute detail of a scene or scenes depicted on the leaf and to relate them to some specific fashion or place: what could be more English than a printed fan of 1795 entitled 'A Collection of Beaus', with its band of 12 vignettes of full-length burlesque figures with titles and appropriate sentences below each one:

The Merry Lover – I live, love and laugh
The Melancholy – I die alas! poor me
The Impetuous – Love! Lend me wings . . .

On the same fan a cupid holds a scroll inscribed 'The Ladies' Bill of Fare or a Copious Collection of Beaux'! This seems to sum up a whole way of living and it contrasts vividly with another printed fan of the same period, which could never be mistaken for an English fan, as it represents uniforms of the Directoire worn by self-conscious members of the French proletariat trying to look sophisticated. Both, however, are quite as relevant from a costume point of view as any fashion print and afford an excellent way of seeing a variety of garments worn at one time.

It is necessary to go back to their earliest origins to comprehend fully the development of fans in Europe. Fans were in use in most ancient cultures, both ceremonially and as useful accessories. Bas-reliefs on the temples of Ancient Egypt show great ceremonial fans carried behind Pharaoh in his chariot, and two such fans were indeed found amongst the treasure of Tutankhamun. They consist of a handle which widens out at the top into a lotus-flower shape, an ornamental semi-circle into which are fixed ostrich feathers. Surviving handles are made of wood, sometimes covered with gold leaf, painted and inlaid with enamel, and bitumen was used to secure the feathers. There is also evidence of smaller, leaf-shaped and other shaped fans, probably made from woven straw or grasses, such as are still in use today in many Eastern countries as accessories for men and women alike. Indeed, in the Middle East, in recent times, it was not unusual to observe men, sitting in cafés sipping tea and coffee, using such fans either to fan themselves or to swat at the flies.

That the fan was an accessory to dress of the elegant Ptolemaic-Alexandrine, there is little doubt.

Tanagra figurines of the Greco-Roman period (c. 200 BC) have a charming fashion quality, showing women in the round, their coiffure, their draperies, their sandals, their hats and sometimes their fans.

Roman ladies had fans, and even the Romano-British are known to have used circular fans. A sculptured tombstone in the Carlisle Museum indicates this quite clearly, showing a lady (c. AD 250) holding a large round fan with radiating ribs; there is further evidence of this type of fan from a fourth-century Roman sarcophagus at York, in which a pair of ivory handles were found and a reconstruction of the object was carried out by archaeologists.[1] It would appear that, from Antiquity onward, the fan in fashion assumed a dual function, that of status symbol, and that of useful ornament.

The transition of the fan from the Middle East to Europe may have occurred in the twelfth century during the period of the Crusades.

An illuminated manuscript of the twelfth century[2] in Berne (Switzerland) shows Louis VII of France on his sick-bed, being fanned by an attendant. The fan depicted in the manuscript could be of Eastern origin. It is not unlike the fans seen in Persian illustrated manuscripts, which are flag-shaped and rigid, consisting of a handle with a frame attached to it at right angles. A similar fan, also flag-shaped, is even more clearly seen in a painting, the Birth of the Virgin (c. 1342, Siena Opera del Duomo), by Pietro Lorenzetti (active 1320-45), and here, the bold pattern of the weaving forms an attractive and very oriental geometrical design. It is perhaps worth noting too that, in both these instances, the fan is used in a sick-room, where it would also serve as a fly swat.

The development of the fixed fan may have been affected by fans brought from South America as part of the Conquistadores' booty, many of which were made of feathers. For example, mention is made of an ornamental feather fan, presented to Queen Isabella of Spain by Christopher Columbus in March 1493, on his return from his first voyage, but the size is not given, and one is left wondering if indeed it may have been a great ceremonial fan or one of the first feather fans which were so fashionable in the sixteenth century.

The feather fan, consisting of various types of plumage on a fixed handle, was the type most commonly in use in Europe in the sixteenth century and in the first half of the seventeenth. The vogue was popularized by Queen Elizabeth I, who carries one in many of her portraits. She appreciated more than most the importance of presenting to the world an image of royalty, and it is therefore hardly surprising to find that she 'wore' a fan extensively. Not only was it a symbol of her majesty (a utilitarian sceptre!), but it could be deemed to be an important accessory to set off and enhance the beauty of those hands of which she was so inordinately (though justifiably) proud.

Furthermore, the softness of the feathers set within the hard, jewelled handle complemented a garment which itself was a combination of light and shade, encrusted with jewels, yet lightened by the finest of veils and the delicate picotee openwork of lace.

1 *Queen Elizabeth I, by an unknown artist, c. 1575.* ▷
The Queen, in her early forties, wears a tawny-coloured gown with looped pearls at her breast. In her right hand she lightly holds the small handle of a feather fan, the colours of which contrast and complement the elegant ensemble.

Portraits of the Queen show her with a variety of fine fans of this type; unfortunately none has survived. This is not surprising, though portraits of her successor, Anne of Denmark, to whom her wardrobe was passed, reveal the re-use of some of the jewelled handles, and some of the fans listed in the Queen's wardrobe list of 1600 are recognizable in her portraits.

Such fans in varying degrees of sumptuousness were in common use at courts all over Europe, and by the late sixteenth century they were carried by the bourgeoisie. John Aubrey, that consummate gossip, writing in the reign of Charles II about the Elizabethan age, describes them thus:

> The Gentlewomen then had prodigious Fannes, as is to be seen in old pictures, like that instrument which is used to drive Feathers: it had a handle at least half a yard long; with these the daughters were corrected oftentimes. Sir Edward Coke, Lord Chief Justice, rode the circuit with such a fan; Mr Dugdale sawe it, who told me of it. The Earl of Manchester used also a Fan. But fathers and mothers slash'd their daughters in the time of that Besome discipline when they were perfect women.

John Aubrey paints an amusing and lively picture, and it is worth noting that men carried fans in an official capacity, the ceremonial aspect percolating, as it were, down through the ages.

While digging on the site of Wakefield House, at the corner of Friday Street and Cheapside in the City of London, in 1912, a workman put his pick through a box which lay beneath a cellar floor. The box, though decayed, contained a large collection of jewellery, most of which is now on display at the Museum of London. Known as the Cheapside hoard, the bulk of this splendid treasure was of jewellery of the Tudor period, most of it Elizabethan. Among the enamelled chains and jewelled pendant earrings on show are a number of objects which have been described as fan handles. They are about 2½ in. (6 cm) in length, mostly enamelled and jewelled, some of them ornamented with fine garnets, amethysts and emeralds and wrought with unusual classical and even Egyptian motifs. They consist of a handle and a hollow cluster at one end which appears to be designed to hold feathers. At the other end is a loop, presumably for hanging from a chain. They are consistent in every way, *except in size*, with known designs of fans in drawings and paintings of the period. Feathers inserted and fixed into these handles could not exceed 2 in. (5 cm) in length, and a fan of an overall size of 4-5 in. (10-12 cm) would hardly tally with John Aubrey's description.

It has been suggested that they are mounts for small tufts of feathers used as hawk lures.[3] Another possibility is that they are indeed fan-holders, albeit in miniature, which, since the Cheapside hoard seems to be the old stock of a journeyman, could in fact be traveller's samples.

Complete fixed feather fans are very rare; only two of them in England have been ascribed to this period. Another one (now lost), formerly at the Musée de Cluny in Paris, is said to have belonged to Gabrielle d'Estrées (1573-99), the favourite of Henry IV, first Bourbon King of France. Designs for fan handles of this period are not uncommon, as can be seen in two elaborate drawings in the Victoria and Albert Museum.

In the same way that gloves were acceptable gifts, even to royalty, so were fans, Queen Elizabeth I being the recipient of many such offerings. Among the gifts presented to Her Majesty on 1 January 1589, the Countess of Bath gave 'a fanne of swanne downe, with a maze of greene velvet, ymbrodered with seed-pearles and a very small chayne of silver gilte, and in the middest a border on both sides of seed pearles, sparks of rubyes and emerods, and thereon a monster of gold, the head and breast mother-of-pearles.'[4]

According to Brantôme, Marguerite de Navarre gave her sister-in-law, Louise de Lorraine, wife of Henry III, a fan made of mother of pearl, ornamented with jewels and large pearls, which was so fine it was thought to be a masterpiece and worth more than 15,000 écus (fig. 2).

Later, fans were to become an integral part of the trousseau of most fashionable brides, while at the same time constituting a charming souvenir of a particular event such as a wedding or a christening. Writing about a wedding day in 1787, Mme de la Tour du Pin recalls the event with true gallic precision:

> . . . Then a footman brought in a large basket of green and gold sword knots, favours, fans and cords for the Bishops' hats, to be distributed among the guests. This was a very costly custom. Sword favours of the finest ribbon cost between twenty-five and thirty francs each. Military sword knots in gold and tasselled cords for the Bishops' hats cost fifty francs, and the fans for the ladies cost between twenty-five and one hundred francs each.

Gifts of this nature continued to be presented on many occasions up till the twentieth century.

It was in the sixteenth century that different types of fans made an appearance in France and, somewhat later, in England. No doubt the wider use of these objects was the result of closer links with Italy brought about by the very political marriage of Catherine of Medici to Henry II of France. She certainly used fans, for Brantôme tells us that when she was widowed in 1559 her heraldic devices included broken mirrors, *broken fans* and severed chains with pearls and beads scattered about.

The Portuguese were the first to establish trade with China and even with Japan and by 1516 they had succeeded in forming a colony in China.[5] The folding fan was by that time, and in a variety of shapes, used both in China and in Japan, from whence it originated.[6] It was this new type of fan which the Portuguese, who had special Papal concessions at this period,[7] must have introduced to Italy by way of the Papal States. As niece of Pope Leo X (a Medici), Catherine of Medici would have been familiar with this latest novelty.

Only in late portraits of Queen Elizabeth I and some of her contemporaries is the folding fan depicted in England. French sources are earlier, and it has always been assumed that this 'new' type of fan had found its way there from Italy. In the famous Ditchley Portrait (National Portrait Gallery, London), Queen Elizabeth I wears a folding fan, the guards (or outer sticks) ornamented with pearls and rosettes, attached to a coral-coloured ribbon which hangs from her waist, a fashion at the same time decorative and practical (fig. 5).

There are several kinds of folding fans, but generally speaking the two principal ones are the pleated fan and the 'brisé' fan.

The pleated fan is composed of a shaped leaf or 'mount' made from a variety of materials, placed over

2 Detail from a tapestry in the series 'Les Fêtes de ▷ Henri III, c. 1580-5. Flemish School. The King is shown with his consort, Louise de Lorraine, who carries a feather fan, the handle of which is as important in size and design as the feathers which are inserted into the complete semi-circular holder attached to a long handle. The feathers are curled and graded.

a set of 'sticks', the outer ones being stouter and usually more highly decorated, and referred to as the 'guards' ('panaches' in French). The base of the sticks may be rounded off or shaped, and contains a pivot which allows for the articulation of the whole fan.

The brisé fan consists of sticks only, held together at the top by a cord or a ribbon, and tapering to the base in which the pivot functions as above.

A feature in two surviving examples of later sixteenth-century pleated fans, one in a private collection, the other at the Musée de Cluny (fig. 4), is the way in which the leaf is attached to the guards; it is threaded into them, and then a rosette or pompon of silk is stitched to the intersection, thus stopping the thread and forming an attractive decoration to the outer sticks. In both fans the sticks are ivory, but the leaves vary, the one having a silk leaf embroidered in coloured silks and gold and silver thread reminiscent of the floral patterns on many late sixteenth-century accessories such as gloves and caps, the other being an interesting combination of vellum with openings filled in with mica and painted with little vignettes representing the legend of Actaeon (fig. 4).

Cesare Vecellio's (1521-1601) splendid book of engravings, *Habiti Antichi e Moderne di Tutto il Mondo,* published in 1598, offers proof of all these fans and others being used in Italy, different States having their preference for this or that type of fan. It is always described as part of the dress, as an accessory, often an indispensable one.

Another type of folding fan is the cockade fan. It can be of the pleated or the brisé kind. Basically it is a folding fan which opens out into a complete circle (but sometimes it only spans a semi-circle) *around*

◁ *3 A late sixteenth-century folding fan of ivory, the double vellum leaf cut out to form a design reminiscent of reticella lace. Mica, pale blue and pink silk, bright blue and green linen and cloth of gold are inserted between the vellum leaves except at the top. French or Italian. (11¾ in. – 300 mm.)*

Plate 4. Fan belonging to Mary Queen of Scots (?) shown at the exhibition of fans at the Drapers' Hall (?)

◁ *4 A folding fan c. 1580 with ivory sticks and guards. The plain guards have six tufts of vermilion silk which hold them to a parchment leaf. The detail shows how the ribs (vermilion-stained) are threaded through the leaf which is further decorated with little 'windows' filled in with mica and painted in black, red, green and gold with figures of gold and silver representing the legend of Actaeon and other motifs typical of French Renaissance decoration. French. (10 in. – 255 mm.)*

---

the pivot. It is designed to be grasped at the base, usually by two handles, which may be held together or clasped by means of a loop or some other device. Cockades went in and out of fashion but their vogue rarely lasted because they were not really practical, and were over ostentatious in use.

An interesting cockade type of fan of pleated silk now in the Museum of Antiquities in Edinburgh, which was part of the Penniquick Collection and is supposed to have belonged to Mary Queen of Scots, could well provide a link through Italy, France, Scotland and England. Mary Stuart was first married to the sickly King, Francois II, Catherine of Medici's eldest surviving son. The handle of the fan under discussion is made of tortoiseshell, which was mainly worked in Italy at that time and indeed exported from there in many forms throughout Europe. The leaf is silk, a fabric not woven in France until two decades later, so it is presumably also Italian. By this time, however, France had absorbed and taken over the lead in fashions from Renaissance Italy.

From the seventeenth century onwards, it is impossible to look at fans in England in isolation, although as fine an English fan could be had as one from anywhere else on the Continent. But many countries, and France above all, played a special role in the history of the fan. If the development of taste in the fashion for fans in England is to be properly understood, the French scene must be carefully consulted and studied in some depth. Huguenot immigrants at the end of the seventeenth century brought their crafts and skills to England, but, above all, from the time of Queen Henrietta Maria, in the early part of that century, French fashions acquired a cachet, almost a 'snob' value for the English, which became synonymous with good taste. No matter how much it was satirized by some, it was avidly absorbed by others.

In the eighteenth century, French fans were so highly regarded that to contravene the English Customs duties, many were run ashore (smuggled in), and not until 1878 was action taken to try to redress the balance.

It was at that time that some influential members of the Worshipful Company of Fan Makers attempted to revive the fan trade in England, which they but partially succeeded in doing, when they held a competitive exhibition of fans at the Drapers' Hall (2-11 July 1878).

By their very nature, and because of the way fans evolved and came to be made in Europe, combining the skills of a great variety of craftsmen, and sometimes those of quite considerable artists, many of them are regarded as minor works of art (as indeed they are), and relatively large numbers have survived because of the loving care of their owners and their descendants. It is all the more surprising, though nevertheless pleasing, that so many of the cheaper, less work-intensive fans can still be found too, in good condition, for they, more than others, constitute those valuable pages of the social story which makes history come to life.

5 Queen Elizabeth I by M. Gheeraerts the Younger,
c. 1592. The monarch wears an elaborate and heavy
garment over a wide hoop. The stiff silhouette,
against a highly symbolic background, is relieved by
delicate touches such as the treatment of the hands,
one holding a pair of gloves and the other a folding
fan, the guards of which are studded with pearls.
The fan is tied to a coral-covered ribbon which is
threaded through the pivot of the fan and attached
to the waist of the dress by the ribbon.

1

The Seventeenth Century

It is impossible truly to appreciate the development of the fan in Europe in the seventeenth century without having some understanding of the political and, by implication, the artistic scene.

Holland, France and England were, by the early seventeenth century, establishing a foothold as the greater trading nations, setting up trading posts throughout the Far East. These countries had succeeded in infiltrating a market hitherto dominated by Italy, Portugal and Spain. It was to Amsterdam, Dieppe and Bristol that ships now came, laden with silks, spices and ivory, rare woods and lacquer ware. One need only consider blue and white Delft-ware with its Chinese origins to realize how much the oriental influence was making itself felt. At the same time, the Renaissance, with its classical overtones, had flowered via Mannerism into the Baroque, a purely Western concept. This two-way current of forms and ideas, which was eventually to blossom into the loosely-termed 'Chinoiserie', had found expression, relatively early on, in the making and wearing of fans, in their shape and overall design.

In 1600 England formed a great trading company, the East India Company (which although so named also traded with China) to exploit and develop trade in the East. England was followed by Holland, and later by France, in setting up rival organizations.[1] The minutes of the East India Company for 1 October 1614 mention paper fans, and by the end of the century Amoy and Canton sold 20,000 fans for export.

Close scrutiny of early seventeenth-century portraits of women carrying folding fans reveals a

6 *Anne Cecil, Countess of Stamford by William* ▷ *Larkin, c. 1615. The slashed white silk gown has a stunning effect against the deep greens of the background and the sumptuousness is emphasized by an outsized handkerchief bordered with magnificent reticella lace and the folding fan of creamy ivory with its fine white kid leaf.*

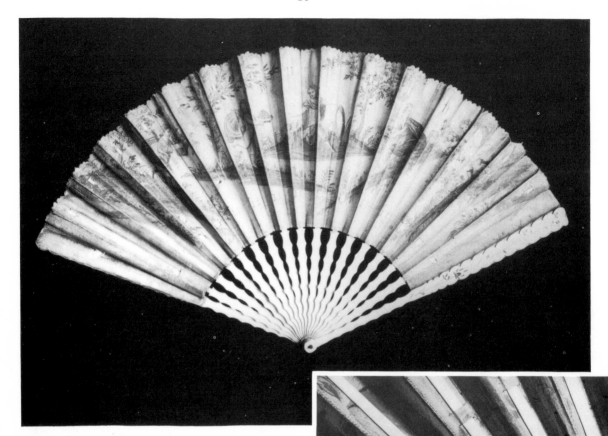

constant factor in their span: they are wedge-shaped, opening at an angle of between 35 to 45 degrees. This certainly suggests an oriental prototype as Chinese fans of this period have the same shape. European manufacturers would have been inspired by oriental models, but fans vary considerably in their length and composition, as well as in the relative proportion of the sticks to the leaf, though there are few surviving fans of this time to confirm the fact.

During the first part of the century women continued to carry feather fans, again of different sizes ranging from small, circular or shaped feathers in black or in bright colours devised to complement an outfit, to two or three long, single coloured plumes set in a handle and sometimes carried by children.

Surviving English and Dutch folding fans, particularly in the earlier part of the century, have a naïve quality which certainly does not exist in their sophisticated Italian and French counterparts. A distinctive feature of some of these fans is the slotting of the sticks into the leaf, as though the fan-maker were treating the vellum or other material used as a textile or wide piece of ribbon (fig. 7).

7 A seventeenth-century fan with ivory sticks and painted guards. The fine skin leaf with its scalloped edge is painted with a mythical figure (possibly Venus) seated on a mound holding a mirror while large, fat putti and an attendant bring offerings of fruit and flowers. Possibly French, c. 1680. (10½ in. — 256 mm). The detail shows the ivory sticks slotted into the leaf and the fine contemporary stitching in the leaf, on the reverse.

There was also a resurgence of the cockade fan (sometimes referred to as a 'parasol fan') with a fabric or vellum mount, sometimes formed from separate cut-out leaf shapes, and rare indeed are the folding fans which do not now display some form of decoration.

The engravings of Abraham Bosse (1602-76) and of Wenceslas Hollar (1607-77) provide one of the best visual sources for the wearing of fans. It would appear from these sources that the feather fan was becoming less fashionable, relegated to the older woman and child and to the smarter tradeswoman; it was the folding fan which had become an essential accessory to the court lady (fig. 8).

Abraham Bosse tells more than most about the lifestyle of French society in the 1630s. Nowhere are the clothes more accurately shown and observed in their minutest detail. It is in prints such as the series of six entitled 'Marriage in the Town' (1633), or the 'Grass Widows at Table' (c. 1635), or the 'Foolish Virgins at Play' (c. 1635) that the 'Précieuses', can be seen. The Marquise de Rambouillet (1588-1665) had set up a select 'salon' at the hotel de Rambouillet in Paris, where the arts and literature were debated. They were mainly female gatherings, and the revival of the old troubadour concept, and an emphasis on platonic love, had the effect of creating a softer fashion, reflected as much in literature as in the deportment and dress of the 'Précieuses'. They were given this name because of their affected mode of speech, resulting in a language of their own: they certainly never 'called a spade a spade', but referred to a fan as 'paravent de la pudeur' (screen of modesty') or an 'utile zephir' ('useful breeze'), describing it by its uses.

Aristocratic court ladies were by no means the only adherents to this fashion, although 'Précieuses'

8a 'Summer' by Wenceslas Hollar (1607-77). An engraving dated 1644 showing a lady fanning herself. The fan appears to be quite large and the design of floral garlands is discernible on the leaf. The sticks and guards are plain and do not reveal any hint of carving or other decoration.

8b 'Autumn' by Wenceslas Hollar. An engraving dated 1644 showing a lady dressed for that season and wearing a small feather fan attached to a ribbon hanging from the waist.

9 Detail of a painting of Diana Cecil, Countess of Elgin, c. 1638, by Cornelius Johnson (1593-1661). The rich blue satin and fine lawn trimmings of her dress leap into life with the only bit of patterning in the picture, the colourful decorations of the fan leaf and painted sticks. A lion passant gules (design inspired by the crest of the Earls of Elgin) can be clearly seen besporting himself among the flowers.

often came from the rapidly growing and increasingly affluent bourgeoisie. A classical education was no longer the prerogative of the sons of noblemen; more and more women were literate and many of them well educated. A far more elaborate subject matter could now be found on the leaves of fans which hitherto had either sought to emulate the intricacies of lace, or merely to form a colourful adjunct to a gown (fig. 9).

Silk, fine kid or vellum was used for fan leaves, with perhaps the added lustre of mica, and gradually flowers and floral subjects were relegated to the reverse of the leaf, while the obverse was treated increasingly as a picture, the subject often copied from, or derived from, known paintings.

10 Tortoiseshell 'landscape' fan, the painted leaf
of fine animal skin with flowers in vivid naturalistic
colours. Of special interest is the double row of
threading which holds the leaf more securely to the
sticks. Dutch or French (second quarter of the
seventeenth century), approximately 15 in. (373 mm).

11 An engraved fan leaf dated 1637, by Abraham
Bosse (1602-76), the central vignette representing
the Judgement of Paris.

It has been seen that Italy was well advanced in the art of fan-making as early as the sixteenth century. Painters such as the Carracci (1557-1602, 1560-1609) are said to have decorated and designed fans at the Villa Monsignori near Bologna, and there are also examples which derive from Domenichino (1581-1641), and could indeed be painted by him.[2]

Favoured subjects came from mythology, the Bible and Roman history and there is little doubt that fine fan leaves as well as the finished objects were exported from Italy throughout Europe. Italian fan leaves were made of finely cured skins of animals, including sables, and they are mentioned in the Venetian sumptuary laws which are quite explicit and detailed.[3]

Among the many subjects to which Abraham Bosse applied his art are a number of fan leaves which he is known to have engraved, possibly with a view to their being coloured or overpainted; also a number of hand-screens have survived in print form. Some of his fan leaves have retained much of their original freshness. Among the subjects are the Judgment of Paris fig. 11, the Birth of Adonis and the Four Ages of Man, subjects with an appeal both to the well-read and to the more mature wearer with a philosophical turn of mind. The artist himself was not beyond a bit of self-advertisement. In the print 'La Galerie du Palais' (fig. 12), he recreates a scene from polite society in the 1630s in Paris, giving a vivid insight into the

shopping habits of the wealthy Parisians: ladies and gentlemen saunter by boutiques, selecting from the books, gloves, collars and lace and discussing fans. A young blood is displaying a fan which appears to cause the admiration of a group of women, while the shopkeeper turns to the shelves to lift down a box clearly inscribed 'Eventails de Bosse' (Fans by Bosse).[4]

Abraham Bosse's artistic career spans the reign of Louis XIII (b.1601, d.1643), whose sister Henrietta Maria was consort to Charles I of England. Few portraits show the Queen holding a fan, and it has been suggested that it was because of her tiny proportions that she is rarely seen with one. Far more plausible is the theory that Van Dyck (1599-1641), court painter to Charles I and a portrait painter above all, may not have wished to include fans: a fine portrait of the Queen by an unknown artist in the National Portrait Gallery (London) shows her holding a folded fan, the leaf of which appears to be of a coral-coloured material. The guard seems to be ivory (it is more yellow-looking than mother-of-pearl which might have been the alternative) and it is studded with pearls. The pivot end is clearly visible in the palm of her hand and it is shaped, while the rivet itself is ornamented with a pearl (fig. 13).

It is, however, to Wenceslas Hollar, an engraver like Bosse, that one must look for a better idea of the cut of dress in England in the first half of the seventeenth century, for hairstyles and above all for detail and accessories such as fans. Born in Prague, Hollar first worked in Frankfurt, Cologne and Antwerp, where he had difficulty to subsist, until Thomas Howard, Earl of Arundel, brought him to England. In 1640 he was teacher of drawing to the Prince of Wales and he fought in the ranks for the King but was captured by Parliament and escaped to Antwerp. He returned to England in 1652 and was appointed His Majesty's Designer in 1660. Before the introduction of photography, engraving was an important profession and, besides making copies of famous paintings, illustrating books and making maps, Hollar engraved a series of pictures of women's costumes — *Muliebris Anglicanus* (1640) and *Theatrum Mulierum* (1643), which have proved invaluable to the historians of

dress. Dating also from this period is a tiny but beautifully detailed engraving entitled 'Muffs and Finery', showing fur muffs, a lace-edged garment, pins, gloves, a mask and two fans, a closed folding fan and a small fixed feather one on a rigid ornamental holder. The etching gives an accurate idea of scale, and the folding fan is certainly longer than the feather one which is much reduced since the early years of the century.

During the mid-seventeenth century, England faced a period of austerity reflected in the sober dress and demeanour of women as prescribed by Cromwell and his followers. Not enough is known about fans in

13 Detail of a painting of Queen Henrietta Maria, attributed to H. van Steenwick, c. 1635. The Queen holds an ivory fan, the leaf of which is of coral-coloured material, the guards studded with pearls. The detail shows well the shaped lower end of the fan in which a pearl surmounts the rivet.

◁ *12 'La Galerie du Palais', an engraving by Abraham Bosse c. 1635. The central boutique specialized in varied fashion accessories which include fans, masks, gloves, muffs, ribbons, favours, necklaces and nightcaps.*

Bosse jn et fe.

14 *An engraving by Abraham Bosse, c. 1633, extolling the virtues of the new sumptuary laws of Cardinal Richelieu prohibiting the lavish use of lace, gold fringe and expensive imports. Prohibition of these articles does not seem to have included fans.*

England at this time, but it is significant that one of the Verney ladies can still write that: 'Kings may be dethroned and Parliaments may totter, but Fashion still rules society with a rod of iron'.[5] In 1633 Richelieu had published an edict against excessive imported luxury goods and superfluous accessories. He did not stop the use of the fan (fig. 14) and it would only be conjecture to suppose that fans were not used in England at the time of Cromwell's dictatorship (1653-58).

It is hardly surprising, however, that after the restoration of the monarchy in 1660, and with such a 'merry' monarch as Charles II, who had spent his years of exile in Holland and France, there was a revival of interest in dress and fans were one of the fashionable accessories to be purchased. The new seventeenth-century society in Britain was free in its choice of clothing. Limitation was due to cost, not to any particular class distinction; but fashionable clothes could be extremely expensive. In 1671 a footman could be earning £4 a year, while in the same year the Third Earl of Salisbury spent £23.6s.6d. for a suit and cloak.[6]

Nor were fans by any means cheap. Bills paid for Elizabeth, Duchess of Somerset, in 1686 list among other items a 'landscape fan' costing £3.8s. – one of the most expensive items on the list, which also mentions another fan at £1.1s.6d., and a price of 1s. 'ffor a culimbine stick to a fane' (this refers to a repair). When the price of a dozen gloves on the same list is £1.10s. and for a 'fine suit with gray lace and gloves' £3.4s.6d., some assessment may be obtained as to the high price set upon a fine fan and its relative value.[7]

Wares were to be bought from small shops located within a larger building. In London goods including gloves, stockings, ribbons, fans, masks and materials could be purchased at the Old or Royal Exchange, or Westminster Hall. The Strand and the Covent Garden area had superseded the City as a fashionable shopping area[8], but garments and other items could be obtained from travelling salesmen who had access to the highest places. In March 1671 Evelyn encountered in the Queen's bed-chamber '. . . a French peddling woman . . . that used to bring fanns and baubles out of France to the Laddys . . .'.

Foreign influences in fans cannot be under-estimated. People were travelling more freely, buying clothes and novelties abroad. Samuel Pepys on 16 May 1660 records that 'This evening came Mr John Pickering on board like an asse, with his feathers and new suit that he had made at the Hague'. Three days later he is there himself buying '. . . some linen to wear against tomorrow . . .' and on 24 May he is 'Up and made myself as fine as I could with Linning stockings and wide Canons that I bought the other day at Hague'.[9]

The King's sister and niece were married in the prosperous Netherlands, and for much of Charles II's reign there was free intercourse with Holland. Catherine of Braganza, Charles II's queen, brought free trade and long lasting ties with her native Portugal and in particular with its eastern colonies. It was the Portuguese who first went to Japan, as early as the fifteenth century. 'Japanned' wares, i.e. lacquer ware, were a most fashionable innovation in seventeenth-century England, to be had in as varied articles as cabinets, chests and fan sticks, which were now being imported in growing quantities. The lure of the exotic East was accessible to many classes of citizen, and Samuel Pepys in 1667 went to an Indian shop near Temple Bar for a loose-fitting 'Indian gown'.[10] Shops of this kind stocked fans which were now specifically being made in the East for export to the European markets.

The main fashionable link was with France through Louise de Kerouaille, one of Charles II's mistresses, the beautiful Duchess of Portsmouth, while the King's youngest sister was married to Louis XIV's brother, 'Monsieur'. France, in the early years of the reign of Louis XIV, the Sun King, with the help of the diligent Colbert had developed and encouraged the arts and their application to commercial uses. Some of the finest skilled craftsmen were Protestants. Political developments and, in 1685, the revocation of the Edict of Nantes by Louis XIV, resulted in an influx of immigrants into the Protestant States of Germany, into Holland and England. Many of these immigrants were talented craftsmen, with fan-makers among them. Something of their background can be learned from the letters patent and statutes drawn up by the Parliament of Paris in April 1670, confirming that by that date the different trades which made some components of fans should be amalgamated into a guild of Fan-makers.[11]

This fascinating set of documents refers to Master guilders on leather wishing to set up in a corporation of Master Fan-makers, ' . . . faiseurs, compositeurs et monteurs d'Eventails, de la Ville, Fauxbourgs et Banlieue de Paris . . . '. Set out in detail are articles by

ÉCOLE FRANÇAISE DU XVIIᵉ SIÈCLE
La MARCHÉ au PAIN et la MARCHÉ à la VOLAILLE
QUAI des AUGUSTINS vers 1670

15 'The Cries of Paris' — one of a series of five painted fan leaves showing the hustle and bustle of life in Paris in the seventeenth century.

which a Master Fan-maker was constrained, which certainly explain why seventeenth-century fans in France may appear to have a restricted subject matter. For example, Article II allows for the painting of birds, flowers, landscapes and people on such varied materials as paper, leather and cloth, but Article III prohibits portraits and pictures, ' . . . ou aucun autre ouvrage de Peinture, que ce qui est propre et sert à faire un Eventail'.

The French Académie, founded in 1648, had a strict hierarchy of members graded according to the subject matter they represented: history painters at the top, portraitists next, and so on, down to land-scape artists. There was no place for the still life or flower painter — this was looked upon as decoration to be used in conjunction with other forms of decor-ative arts. In order to ensure against infringement of their statutes in Article III, the Jury of Master Painters and Sculptors were allowed to go to the Master Fan-makers to verify that they had complied with the rules (and this at no cost to themselves — the expense presumably to be borne by the Fan-makers).

Documents such as these are the more exciting when it is possible to relate them to objects such as the vivid series of fan leaves in the Carnavalet Museum in Paris dating from the 1670s.[12] It would seem that among permitted themes were genre subjects, and these depict in detail scenes in the thriving city (fig. 15). A lively river scene on the Seine, with the Quai de la Mégisserie in the background, shows how the Parisian laundries functioned in the seventeenth century. No special skill is needed to detect the hierarchy, both in trades and conditions of the people depicted, from the lowly washerwoman and the apprentice to the fat fishwife, the smart shop-owner, the busy bourgeois, the elegant lady. Dress-wise it is hard to find more complete visual documentation, and it is tempting to wish for another fan leaf which might have shown the mysteries of fan-making. It is not until the following century that these are fully revealed.

However, from this series of fan leaves, and other surviving examples it does appear that the French fan-makers adhered to the statutes mentioned above. Religious themes and great historical subjects were the prerogative of the painters and do not appear as such on the leaves of French fans; even topical subjects are treated in a semi-allegorical style, while Biblical and historical subjects are treated as theatrical performances. Examples of this exist in the British Museum (and in the Victoria and Albert Museum, where the fan is the more interesting as it is mounted on tortoiseshell). This is a large fan, and it has a lush quality which is in keeping with the somewhat upholstered look of the dresses of the period. The people in this genre scene, which depicts the toilet of a nobleman, are replaced by elderly-looking putti whose presence seems to be a *sine qua non* in most French fans other than the purely topographical. Putti were, in fact, regarded as purely ornamental forms and their presence turns a historical subject such as the marriage of Louis XIV (colourplate 1) into a decorative theme; it is as though the little amorini and other motifs incorporated into the borders of the earlier Bosse fans (fig. 11) have burst their confines and taken over.

On Italian fans subject matter was unrestricted and sticks and guards became increasingly elaborate. Piqué-work and fine inlay ornament the tortoiseshell, mother-of-pearl and ivory employed in stick making. These fans were appreciated as much in England as in France.

It would not be an overstatement to conclude that the first half of the seventeenth century in Europe was a transition period for the fan, but that, in the second half of the century, the folding fan, in its different shapes, finally achieved the status of adjunct to the dress of any lady of quality, and was indeed, by the end of the century, an integral part of her wardrobe.

---

16   An Italian fan, the ivory sticks and guards ornamented with piqué work and applied mother-of-pearl. The fine kid leaf is well painted in the classical manner; the scene depicts Pan with Syrinx about to be changed into a clump of reeds. Freedom of handling and sophistication are the hallmarks of this fan. c. 1710-20.

2

The Eighteenth Century

If the eighteenth century is referred to as the 'Age of Enlightenment', then, fan-wise, it must be the age of breezes! No dress occasion was complete without the fan, and by the beginning of the century a clear pattern of trade and manufacture had been established.

Enlightenment is indeed the key expression, for it is in the eighteenth century that the great dictionaries appear, listing and illustrating everything in alphabetical order. Social comment is rife, not only in private diaries, but in poems and other forms of literature, and not least on the pages of the rapidly growing and popular newspapers and periodicals. The emergence of the middle-classes into an ever-more powerful social force is a major contributory factor to the vulgarization of many items hitherto the province of only the very rich or of the aristocracy.

In England, the fan-makers, many of whom, as has been mentioned, were émigrés from France, formed themselves into a corporation in 1709, the Worshipful Company of Fan Makers, which still exists.[1] This was partly as a result of the difficulties which arose from competition between English fans and imported ones. At the start of the Company, between 200 and 300 people were involved in the business of fan-making and applied for membership. In April 1709, when the Worshipful Company of Fan Makers was granted its charter, its main function was to protect the trading and manufacture of fans in England, 'so that the Guild might control, watch and curtail the activities' of all those involved in the trade, which was divided, as it were, into sub-trades, listed as 'fan-maker', 'stick-maker', 'ribbon-weaver', and 'fan-painter'.[2] It may be noted too that, at the time of its formation, the Worshipful Company of Fan Makers appointed a separate warden to control the 'foreigners' — French and Italian, some of whom were genuine masters of the trade, but who also included a number of speculators.

Many fans were still imported from the East, mostly sold via the East India Company through the port of Canton.[3] On various occasions the fan-makers protested at the importation of these fans, going as far as to demand a prohibition order. Petitions and protests continued throughout the eighteenth century without very much success. The Court Minutes of the East India Company in 1752 noted that an appeal from the fan-makers was heard and sent back to them, and a report of the petition appears in Felix Foley's *Bristol Journal*:

> On Wednesday . . . a great number of Poor Fan-stick Makers and others, occupying different Branches of the Fan Trade, presented a Petition to the said Court setting forth the great Hardships they laboured under by the Importation of India Fans, the chief part of which, by being run ashore, pay neither Duty nor Indulgence, and most of which are retailed at Six Pence each, to the Prejudice of the Petitioners, who have been regularly bred to the trade of Fan-Making, and have no other Means to support themselves or and Families . . . .

A complicated set of rates and customs dues on imported fans, whether from the Continent of Europe or from the East, made them liable to duty, but this does not seem to have deterred them from finding their way into England.

Some idea of the quantities of imports can be had from extracts from the India Office series of China Factory Records between 1721 and 1738. These comprised the seasonal diaries of the supracargoes (supracargoes were the 'middlemen' who verified, registered, received and then allowed the sale of cargoes at the port of arrival of a ship). There are numerous mentions of fans:

> On 15 December 1721:
> the supracargoes of the Frances received the following Register of Goods from Capt., Newsham, viz:
>
> 15 Chests, 60 Tubs China Ware
> 4 Screens
> 1 pr. Cabinets
> 1000 Fans.

On 17 December 1721:
Private trade belonging to Peter Godfrey Junr. on board the Cadogan, Captn. John Hill:

    a Tub
    a Small Chest
    a Box   China Ware
    a Box Fanns

Private Trade belonging to James Elwick on board the Frances, Captn. Thos. Newsham.
    one Chest of China Ware
    one Chest of China Ware
    a Parcell of fanns and Lackered Ware . . . .

It is not certain whether these notes refer to mounted fans, or sets of fan sticks, or indeed brisé fans which are made up of sticks only. Brisé fans form one of the most important groups imported from China and they were popular throughout the period. They were usually of carved and pierced ivory, worked to a maximum degree of finesse, lace-like in their delicacy and matching the light muslins and cottons which were in fashion by the end of the century. They were being shipped to England via Canton.

Not all brisé fans were made at Canton. Another important source was the Imperial Ivory Works at

17   A so-called Vernis-Martin ivory brisé fan, the guards and gorge decorated in the Chinoiserie manner, the main part depicting the sacrifice of Iphigenia. The reverse is painted with a very Dutch-like landscape. Probably Dutch, 1710-20.

Peking. The early eighteenth-century imported ivory brisé fans present some curious and quite distinctive features. They seem to have been made specifically for the European market and in contemporary sources they are often referred to as 'India fans' because they came via the East India Company. The genre subjects which ornament them are treated in much the same way as procelain decoration, the figures having a naive quality which is quite alien to oriental native crafts.

In particular, the dress of the figures is often misrepresented so that it is evident that the artist is interpreting a model with which he is not too familiar;[4] he was, no doubt, working from a print or engraving, the subject of which must have appeared incomprehensible, since European mythology and contemporary illustrations of novels and plays were often used. All these brisé ivory fans are identical on both sides, the transparency of the fine ivory blades allowing for a tracing to be made on the other side. The earlier ones are usually threaded at the top with a fine cord, and not, like their European-made counterparts, held together with a ribbon. Only towards the end of the century were they assembled in Europe. Then little cartouches were often left blank for a miniature subject, shield shapes which are purely European were incorporated into the all-over design to hold initials, and a fine ribbon was threaded into the uppermost part of the sticks; these fans varied in size and span to conform with European fashions in fans.

In the first quarter of the eighteenth century, brisé fans, whether oriental or European, can be clearly seen to belong to groups or categories — though invariably there will be the odd exception. In Europe they were painted and decorated with the type of mythological or historical scene familiar from painted fans of the seventeenth century (fig. 17). They are often called 'Vernis Martin', after the Martin brothers who invented a special type of light varnish used on small items of furniture, coach panels etc. Although they are indeed varnished and were sometimes revarnished by well-meaning 'restorers' in the following century, the claim to the famous Vernis Martin name is so far unsubstantiated for there is no mention of fans in any of the Martin inventories.

Among the distinctive features of another group of early brisé fans is an elegant scroll fretwork of carved ivory, often left unadorned, forming a background to the vignettes which make up the main part of the fan. In nearly every case the gorge (the lower part of the sticks) is decorated separately in a different idiom. 'Chinoiserie' is the most favoured, but pseudo-Persian can also be found, while the guards are hatched and display a male or female figure, the female figure often carrying a large fan; there may also be a recognizable flower or fruit. The quality of painting varies from the superb to the indifferent, or at any rate to the mechanical. This type of fan is far more likely to have been made in Holland than in France from where it has been supposed they came.

Holland had, at that time, a thriving fan industry. Centred in Amsterdam, the fan trade was conducted from specialized shops of which there were quite a number.[5] Many French craftsmen had settled in Holland and they were in no way restricted as they had been in their native country. With the freedom that ensued it was possible to give out some of the work to people with lesser skills, working at home, so that a kind of cottage industry grew up, which dealt with the minor forms of decoration such as the reverse of fan leaves. These reverses were painted with a 'semis', a scattering of flowers of the type seen on textiles or porcelain, or with a sketch-like wash of a very simplified building, or a building in a landscape in watercolour. Another form of decoration was the adornment of the leaf (or the sticks in the case of a brisé fan), with stick-on spangles of punched gilt paper, the motifs of these spangles being as varied as tiny putti, kings' or queens' heads, busts, birds, flowers and baskets of fruit.

It is possibly to the ivory brisé fan that Alexander Pope refers in 1711, in *The Rape of the Lock* (canto V):

"To arms, to arms!" the fierce virago cries
And swift as lightening to the combat flies.
All side in parties, and begin th'attack;
Fans clap, silks rustle, and tough whalebones crack;

A 'clap' is a sound more likely to be heard when an all ivory fan is closed in a hurry. The same poem (canto III) vividly evokes the atmosphere of the time:

Hither the heroes and the nymphs resort,
To taste awhile the pleasures of the Court,
In various talk th'instructive hours they past,
Who gave the ball, or paid the visit last;
One speaks the glory of the British queen,
And one describes a charming Indian screen;
A third interprets motions, looks and eyes;
At ev'ry word a reputation dies.
Snuff, or the fan, supply each pause of chat,
With singing, laughing, ogling, and all that.

By the middle of the century the pleated fan was more commonly used than the ivory brisé and the feather fan, or an apology for such in the shape of two or three plumes, is only seen in fancy dress, masque or theatrical costume. This touches too upon the duality of the fan as a mask and, although there are indeed fans which contain little gauze or gut covered observation slits, there are a few which actually combine the two uses. There are seven examples known to date of a rare English printed fan (*c.* 1740) which incorporate a face, or mask, in the centre of the leaf, the reserves (the spaces on the outer sides of a fan leaf) being filled in with scenes of contemporary life. One scene depicting the interior of a fan shop with a prominent display of mask fans is of particular interest.

The best known contemporary description of the manufacture of the pleated fan is to be found in the section entitled 'Eventailliste' ('Fan-maker') from Diderot's *Encyclopédie* of 1765, with plates showing in detail and at every stage the process of fan manu-

18a 'La Déclaration' by de Troy, 1731. A conversation piece in which every detail of dress is observed.
The proportion of the fans and the way they are held
are especially worth noting.

18b Detail from La Déclaration' by de Troy'. The
closed fan is held loosely, in the manner of a cigarette.

facture in France and it is likely that the techniques depicted are similar to those used for manufacture in England. It has been pointed out that the workers are all women.[6] By this time the statutes regarding fan-making had relaxed, not only to permit women workers, but even to include widows of fan-makers as members of the Guild and, provided they did not remarry, they were eligible to a pension.

Plate I, entitled 'Eventailliste, Colage et Préparation des Papiers', shows the interior of a workroom where the paper which serves to make fan leaves is prepared, and figures 1 to 6 show the process by which it is stretched over a frame in pairs. At the bottom of the plate the ruler to scales in '4 pieds' with divisions is shown (fig. 19a).

Plate II, captioned 'Eventailliste, Peinture des Feuilles', features another room where a woman is copying a design set up on the table in front of her in a semi-circular frame. Beneath the picture figures 1 and 2 show the prepared leaf on a board; figure 3 shows the paint brushes, figures 4 and 5 the paint box and shell which serves as a palette to mix the colours, figure 6 a receptacle for water (the paints used were a form of water colour), figure 7 the fan case (for the picture to be copied), figures 8 and 9 the compass or calipers, and again, at the bottom of the page, is the scale ruler, '3 pieds' with 12 divisions (fig. 19b).

Plate III, entitled 'Eventailliste, Monture des Feuilles', shows two women at work in a well-lit room, with windows on either side and two cupboards in the background. Beneath the picture, figure 1 shows the painted leaf and indicates that it is a double leaf. Figures 2 and 3 show the grooved walnut

19 'Eventailliste', from Diderot's Encyclopédie *(1765) showing the stages of fan-making in eighteenth-century France.*

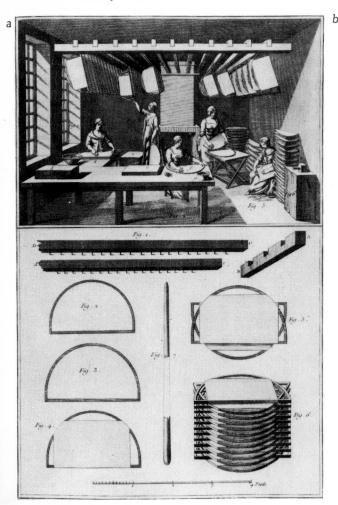

a

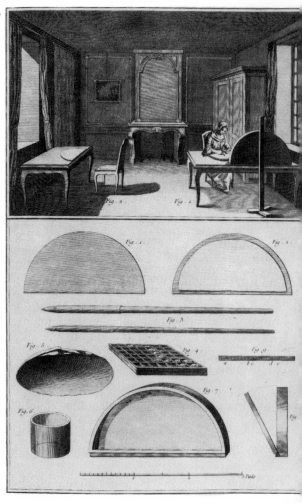

b

wooden board, upon which, in figures 4 and 5, the leaf is placed. Explanations are given for the correct positioning of the leaf, and special care is advocated to keep parts of the design on the flat, i.e. faces or relevant designs should not be on the inside part of a pleat. The leaf is clamped down (fig. 5a) and scored along the radiating lines of the board with a small instrument (fig. 5d) shown in figures 6 and 7. Again the ruler of '3 pieds' features at the foot of the page (fig. 19c).

Plate IV, captioned 'Eventailliste, Monture des Eventails', shows the final stages of fan-making, with the removal of the leaves from the board, ensuring that the insertions are free to take the sticks (fig. 11), trimming (figs. 12 and 13), inserting the sticks (fig. 14), top trimming (fig. 15) and finally ribboning the top of the leaves (fig. 16) together, thus keeping the double leaf in permanent position. Figure 17 shows the finished article, and in this plate the ruler

does not appear (fig. 19d).

Other articles in the *Encyclopédie* shed light on the techniques used in making fans, particularly the one on the craft of the 'tabletier' who manufactured sticks and guards, an important and costly part of the fan. Tabletier does not seem to have a satisfactory translation — toy-man or fancy-goods maker being the nearest word in the dictionary.

Another edition, in 1783, the *Encyclopédie Methodique — Arts et Metiers,* or Arts and Crafts, in describing the art of the 'tabletier' (Volume 8), adds 'piquer et incrusteur de tabatiéres et autres ouvrages [other works] ' defines the art of piqué-work. Briefly, a drawing was made which was transferred to the tortoiseshell or other material to be used. Little holes were then traced through by hand and gold and silver wire drilled into the holes which formed the design. The wire was then cut away, and the host material heated. This expanded the hole while at the

d

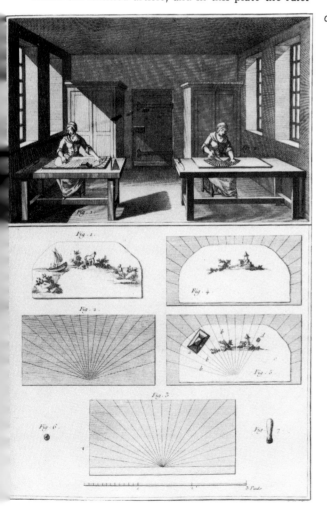

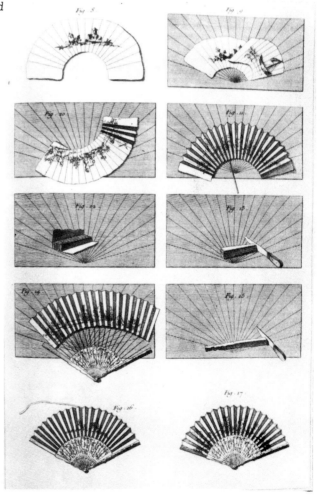

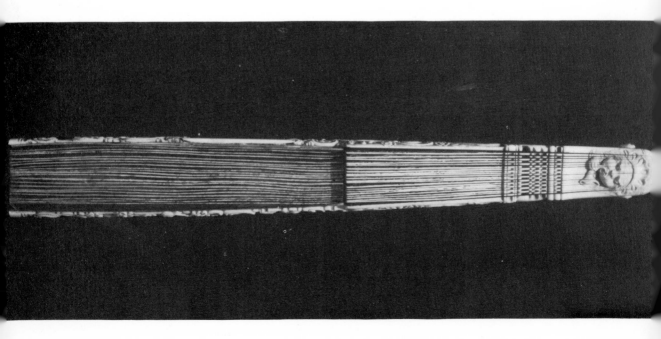

20a A fine fan, c. 1750s; the carved, pierced and painted ivory sticks are decorated with frolicking bacchantes and the paper leaf is painted with a classical scene depicting the abduction of Helen, within the border of flowers and fruit.

same time melting the metal, and, on cooling down, it tightened up, thus holding fast the metal wire which had spread over the perforation, forming a tiny screwhead. This form of decoration was used on fan sticks and guards in the seventeenth century and was in vogue in the early eighteenth century. The article goes on to mention that according to a law passed on 11 August 1776 the 'tabletiers' were incorporated into the Guild of Lute-makers and Fan-makers.

In Volume 2, under the heading 'Eventailliste' it is stated that sticks and guards are made by the master 'tabletier', while it is the 'fan-makers' who fold the leaves, assemble the fans and sell them. This indicates conclusively that sticks and leaves were made in different establishments and by different workers, subject to differing rules, according to their guilds — the trade unions of the eighteenth century.

Fan sticks and guards were made from many materials and 'tabletiers' worked in wood (of different sorts, indigenous to Europe like box, or imported such as sandalwood), in bone, tortoiseshell (which was costly), horn, mother-of-pearl (a difficult substance to carve and pierce) and in the eighteenth century, in France and England, mainly in ivory. Already, in 1723, Savary des Bruslons was commenting that English fans were in every way as fine, if not superior, particularly in the ivory carving, to their French counterparts.[7]

It is often the design and disposition of the sticks and guards and their relationship to the leaf which help to date an eighteenth-century fan, and generally speaking these elements fluctuate more in accordance with the fashionable architectural proportions than with the change in the cut of dress. The leaves relate more to textiles and reflect the colours in vogue, though having multi-coloured subjects they could adapt to a variety of outfits.

In 1789 Mme de la Tour du Pin describes her Court

20b The same fan closed, showing the pattern made by the carved sticks and the handle knob which forms a stylized head, the cheeks puffed and blowing into a horn. (11½ in. — 290 mm.)

presentation outfit and says: ' . . . my gloves were trimmed with blue ribbons, my fan was of a similar shade, and there were blue feathers in my hair'. But it was so unusual to have all matching accessories that it was remarked upon. In some fans, sticks, guards and leaf are *en suite*, but it is not always easy to study a fan as 'one piece', because there are many instances where the mounts and sticks have been reassembled at different times and periods.

Shapes and proportions of stick to leaf varied, as did the shapes of the sticks themselves. In the first half of the century the sticks overlapped each other in the gorge of the fan, forming a solid plain or carved and decorated surface when the fan was open. By the 1760s a more open design appeared, the thinner sticks spaced widely apart, the leaf often at this period being quite narrow. The term for this arrangement of the sticks is a 'monture squelette'.[8]

Where the sticks are of the 'battoir' kind they do not overlap but are shaped like a bat, a tennis racket or a violin. Sometimes the bat shape alternated with a plain stick, but the sticks were always highly adorned, pierced, carved and gilt, with designs which derived from furniture motifs of decoration. By the 1770s fans could and did reach their maximum span, opening out at an angle of 180°. They are known as 'eventails de plein vol'.

Diderot's *Encyclopédie* shows the making of a paper or parchment fan, with a double leaf. Other materials were used for the leaf, such as fine vellum, kid and later silk, cotton and linen. When the leaf was made from animal skin it was seldom double, the upper part of the sticks or ribs being visible on the reverse. Even though this is termed 'monture à l'Anglaise' this way of attaching the leaf to the sticks is also found in early Italian fans where the ribs are ornamented with a distinctive wavy line in metallic paint, more often corroded and showing as a green line. The best fan leaves were painted, and commanded the highest price, and the most expensive were those with fine painted leaves on elaborate sticks, the guards sometimes containing real jewels; but there were cheaper fans too.

Prices quoted in the *Encyclopédie Methodique* of 1783 are from 15 deniers (very cheap) each to 30 to 40 'pistoles' (the pistole was a gold coin). Less good or mediocre fans might be sold by the gross, the fine quality fans being retailed singly. Top quality fans might be worth up to 10 livres each and attract high duties, while the run of the mill fan was categorized as haberdashery.

At the beginning of the eighteenth century, Italy was still selling fans to France, mostly of fine scented

21 Madame de Céran, signed and dated 1754 by Jean-Marc Nattier (1685-1766). The fan with its undulating sticks forming a distinctive design in the flat of the lower end is typical of that period and echoes the Rococo shell shape of the lady's cuffs and bodice.

22 A fine French fan, c. 1765, with mother-of-pearl sticks and guards, carved, pierced and painted. The painted paper leaf shows a pastoral party in progress. The coiffure of the dancing lady is not unlike that of Signora Baldrighi in fig. 23, and the seated lady on the right is fanning herself with a fan, the dimensions of which are roughly those of the one on which she is depicted. ($10\frac{1}{3}$ in. – 265 mm.)

skins, but by the middle of the century the fan industry there was adapting to suit the demands of the increasing influx of travellers from all over Europe, including Britain. At first, Italy favoured the mythological subjects, usually derived from well known paintings. Guido Reni's 'Aurora' is often repeated (with variations on the theme) throughout the century, this being a painting admired, not only by the Italians, but by the now rapidly growing flow of visitors on the Grand Tour.[9]

Rome and Naples were both centres for the production of the popular tourist fan, with its views of the ruins of antique Rome or Vesuvius in eruption, bordered with motifs and Pompeian designs, the themes and treatment running in close conjunction with the mosaic jewellery. At least one of these fans is inscribed with the name and full address of the fan-shop in Naples (fig. 25).[10]

Fan leaves continued to be painted in Italy and brought home by visitors in specially designed folders to be mounted or simply to be preserved on their

◁ 23 Self portrait of the artist and his wife c. 1765 by Giuseppe Baldrighi (1723-1802). Signora Baldrighi is dressed in her best, in a fine silk gown with a buttoned stomacher. Her flowers and ribbons, her fan and her pets all point to her status in society: the smart wife of a fashionable portrait painter. All the accessories in this double portrait are exuberant, in keeping with the Latin temperament of the wearers.

own merit.[11] This may have been a way of avoiding the duties imposed upon imported fans. Sometimes the leaves were mounted on the finest Chinese imported sticks and presented as gifts. Nor were such gifts mere trifles. Horace Walpole (1717-97) on various occasions sent fans through his friend James Mann to ladies of quality while he was in Italy. In 1740 he requested Mann to keep some fans he had purchased for the Princess de Craon till he reached Florence, and again in November 1741 he bought more for her. In May 1742 Madame Galli is 'vastly pleased with her

24 A Louis XVI fan with ivory sticks and guards pierced, carved and gilt. The sticks form elaborate designs with three medallions, while carved putti hold up the brightly painted leaf at alternate sticks. (French, c. 1775) (10¾ in. − 273 mm.)

fan', and on 21 July 1742 he is again 'buying fans for princesses at Florence'.

J. Berry mentions prices in 1784: 'Rome . . . to a painter of fans. Bought two of the ruins of Rome for a sequin apiece', a sequin being, at that time, the price of six pairs of fine gloves.[12]

Most countries in Europe were developing their own techniques, but looking over their shoulder as it were, for the results, on the whole, are not dissimilar. Even northern countries like Sweden had fan-makers, the fashion-conscious woman's requirements having to be catered for at all levels and in all climates![13] Signatures on eighteenth-century fans are very rare and, if any, they are always suspect at a first glance. It was not until the nineteenth century that either the producers or the consumers thought fit to record their authorship.

Fan painting and decorating, like embroidery also became a pastime for the leisured, talented lady, and, as with that art, pattern books such as the *Ladies' Amusement* by Jean Baptiste Pillement (1719-1808) were circulated and could provide permutations of the same designs for decorating and ornamenting fans, chinaware and all manner of textiles.[14] Queen Marie Antoinette (1755-93) signed and painted a fan in 1786[15] and the Princess Elizabeth, daughter of George III of England, is known to have decorated a number of fans and was indeed a competent artist.

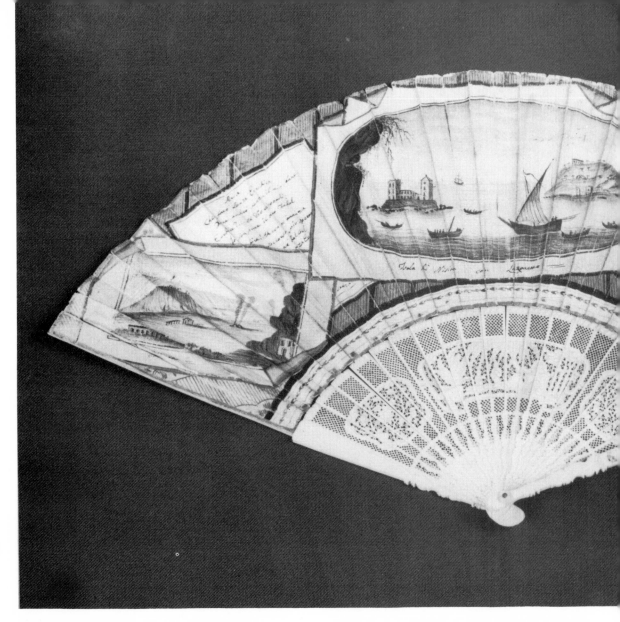

25 A carved ivory fan, typical of Chinese export
work, with a fine skin leaf painted with three trompe
l'oeil views of the environs of Naples upon a ground
of grey and pink, with two leaves of handwritten
script placed between. On one, beneath the caption
'Aria', are words from the opera Orpheus and
Euridice. The other leaf gives the name and address of
the painter, Sign. Nicola Lanezno, and is dated Naples,
1779. This is a good example of a typically 'tourist'
Italian leaf, probably mounted up in England on fine,
imported Eastern sticks. It is said to have belonged to
Queen Charlotte (1744-1818), consort of George III.
(11¾ in. – 270 mm.)

In France the subject most favoured on fan leaves
was the 'fête galante' or 'fête champetre', and it is a
theme which carried on throughout the century in
one form or another, be it as an idealized marriage
party with the altar of Hymen and cupids and garlands
of flowers, or as some literary reference, or simply an
elegant gathering in a country setting. As the century
progressed little vignettes of courtly life formed the
subject of the paintings on the silk leaves which come
into vogue in the 1770s: fashionable ladies in large
hats play with a child or children in a well-ordered
park, with a loving husband or an 'abbé' in attend-
ance. These silk fans provide too a background for
sewn-on spangles and by the end of the century the
vignettes have disappeared in favour of swirls and

classical designs made up of spangles which catch the light and glitter, an accessory much needed by the 'fast' Merveilleuses of the Directoire, with their pretensions and aspirations to classical beauty.

English fans of this period have much in common with the French ones, while retaining an unmistakably English character. The posed vignettes of French or even Austrian ladies enjoying the 'simple' life in tight gowns and elegant coiffures were replaced by rather more formal shaped medallions, often of printed satin, derived from engravings of paintings by Reynolds, Morland, Angelica Kauffmann and other fashionable artists. Also their disposition or placing within the leaf is more sparse, and they are, on the whole, very much less colourful than their Continental counterparts.

Topicality was never far removed from the leaves of fans, and, recording the conquest of Space in 1783, there are smart ballooning fans. Others, all slightly different, refer to the high hairstyles which came in about 1775. When Marie Antoinette sent her mother a miniature portrait of herself dressed in the latest fashion in 1775, the Empress of Austria returned it, saying that some mistake must have occurred, for this was not the portrait of her daughter, but of some actress![16] Caricatures of this fashion abound, in France, England and Germany, and on the leaves of fans the paintings derive from these caricatures,[17] with the hairdresser mounted on a ladder and the gentlemen observing the contraption through a telescope! One of these fans is captioned: 'la Folie des Dames de Paris' (col. pl. 3). The ladies' dressing cape, the combs, the pomatum pot, the curling tongs, all are minutely observed, and these fans are as much documents of fashion as fashion accessories! Even greater topicality is seen on printed fan leaves.

There is a close connection too with the authors of fashion plates, and several engravers, such as B. Picart (1673-1733) who in the first part of the century inspired groups of figures, and Daniel Chodowiecky (1726-1801), engraving for the German almanacs in Berlin in the 1770s and 1780s, are also known to have printed fan leaves.

By the 1750s large numbers of printed fans were in circulation, every possible subject being an inspiration, the more topical the better. As early as 1733, advertisements from Gamble and Pinchbeck appeared in London newspapers for 'Royal Wedding Fans' to celebrate the marriage of Princess Anne, daughter of George II, to William, Prince of Orange, a wedding which did not take place until March of the following year (4 March 1734).

1734 saw the passing of the Copyright Act. This meant that in England printed fans were required to bear the name, address and date of publication. However, these are not always visible for they could be trimmed away when mounting the leaf on to the sticks. Where the dates do exist, of course, the fans are of considerable historical interest.

The French had been engraving fan leaves in the previous century when they had been prized luxury goods and were without a doubt used as the basis for some of the finer painted fans; it is not until the eighteenth century that this method was used in England and Germany, with the difference that fans of this type came in the less expensive end of the range.

Lady Charlotte Schreiber (1812-95) concentrated her collection of fans and fan leaves (now in the British Museum) on the printed fan, and a cursory perusal of the catalogue of this collection by Lionel Cust is sufficient to see that, not only did most of the well-known engravers print fans, but by the end of the eighteenth century, England, Holland, Germany and France were all engraving fan leaves and exporting them to one another. On English fans, names such as Sarah Ashton, F. Chassereau, Gamble, Clarke, J. Cock and J.P. Crowder, Lewis Wells, etc., show the designing and publication of such fans to have been a thriving business.

Techniques on printed fans were varied and included line engravings, woodcuts, stipple-engravings, etchings, etc.; they might be coloured by hand.

As for subjects, they are endless. Biblical and classical subjects are represented, pastoral, social, instructive and plain fancy, but perhaps the most interesting are the historical ones. This last category includes the Coronation of George II in 1727 (before the passing of the Copyright Act), the fireworks of 1749 with a view of a temporary building erected in Green Park for the celebrations marking the signing of the Peace of Aix la Chapelle (October 1748), a lampooning of the European War of 1757, many references to George III, and the trial of Warren Hastings in 1788.

26 A printed English fan leaf, illustrating the interior of the Pump Room at Bath. The design is a copper engraving by George Speren, with a light wash which brings out the wealth of detail in the dress of the men and women, nearly all of whom carry a fan and wear a black hat elegantly perched atop a white cap. c. 1737.

By the end of the century the evidence of fashion plates shows large, relatively simple forms of fans in vogue. Often they were the printed ones with their political messages, for they were cheap and accessible to most pockets.

The development of the printed fan meant that everyone, from the noble lady to the most modest middle-class woman, now carried a fan. It is said that Charlotte Corday was carrying a fan in one hand, while she plunged a knife into Marat.[18] Revolutionary fans read like a history book: 'The taking of the Bastille' (1789), 'Les Droits de l'Homme' (1789), 'La

28 A wooden fan of the French Revolution, c. 1795, ▷ with darker wooden guards and applied ivory on the pivot end. The double paper leaf is printed with a trompe l'oeil of assignats (money orders); the reverse is plain blue paper.

27 A fashion plate dated 1797 from Costume ▷
Parisien *showing clearly the sparse decoration on the
fan.*

Liberté', 'Le Serment Critique' (1789), 'La Fête de la Fédération' (1790), 'La Soirée des Poignards' (1791), 'La République Française', 'Petion' (1791), 'Constitution', 'Mirabeau', 'Assignats' (fig. 28), 'Marat and Lepelletier' (1792), 'Marat, Lepelletier, Charlier and Baras', 'Capture of Toulon' (1793), 'Fête de l'Etre Suprême' (1794), 'Costumes of the Revolution', 'Notre Dame de Lorette' (after 1797), 'Siége d'Anvers', 'Napoleon Bonaparte'. Each inexorable step is marked by a fan, and the opposition too had patriotic fans, faithful to the memory and in honour

of the beheaded monarchs, issued in England, Germany and Austria, but printed in French.

The French Revolution in 1789 marked the end (for a time) of the elaborate confections which had been the prerogative of the French fan-makers, and which are associated with them. Trade embargoes and the economic state of the country precluded the importation of goods such as ivory, and most revolutionary fans have bone or wooden sticks.

Although the social and economic climate was somewhat different in England, it was nevertheless reflected in the fan leaf. Alongside the printed fan, some of the most beautiful ivory imports come into their own, exquisitely pared (fig. 29) and carved to resemble a fine embroidered muslin which was being worn by the most fashionable women. Fashions die hard, and there are still spangle-embroidered fans with perhaps a printed satin medallion incorporated into the leaf, but the general design is more often less dense, in keeping with lighter garments such as the chemise dress of the 1780s.

29 An ivory brisé fan, c. 1795, pierced and carved in the Orient for an English lady. The gorge contains a shield shape with entwined initials, and two doves support the central medallion which is a painted miniature of a frigate flying the British Ensign, lying off a tiny tropical island, complete with palm trees and a lighthouse. (10 in. – 250 mm.)

30 An ivory fan, c. 1789, entitled 'On the King's Happy Recovery'. An elegant, restrained and very English Georgian fan commemorating the restoration to health of George III on one of the many occasions when the monarch recovered from a fit of illness. The white paper leaf is painted and the deep blue border is inscribed: 'health is restored to One and happiness to millions'.

31 A typically English wooden fan with plain sticks and guards, the printed leaf designed to commemorate the escape from assassination of George III at Drury Lane on 13 May 1800, an incident featured on the left-hand side of the fan. Compared with the earlier Georgian fan (fig. 30), the new fashionable shape is easily discernible, with the wider leaf and closer sticks in a narrow gorge. (10½ in. – 267 mm.)

Mezzotints after Angelica Kauffmann (1741-1807) and other popular artists of the late eighteenth century decorate fan leaves, as well as the wooden brisé fans, and miniature copies of their designs are inserted in the shape of vignettes into ivory brisé fans of this period.

With the large ivory fan one may contrast the brisé sandalwood fan, threaded through with a characteristic parti-coloured silk ribbon, sometimes cleverly ornamented with prints stuck onto either side of the fan sticks to open four ways, revealing a different picture at each opening. They are known as puzzle fans or two-way fans, and certainly had their origin in the East.

England's isolation during the French Revolution and then at the time of hostilities with Napoleon — communications being what they were — obliged women, to a certain extent, to evolve a mode of dress which was particular to themselves, and there is as much an English style of dress and fans as there is a French one.

Despite the improprieties of court life and dress in the time of the Regency and George IV, English fashions appear sober beside the sartorial reaction to the horrors of the Revolution in France. The 'Merveilleuses' of the Directoire (1795-99) draped themselves 'à l'antique', attended dubious parties, their febrility matched by their bright trinkets. Fans varied considerably in size, but they were designed to catch the light and sparkle, and more than ever before they were a complement to the dress (or non-dress) of the wearer.

During the eighteenth century, fans were seldom furnished with a loop on the pivot end. The pivot could, however, contain a watch or even a tiny snuff box. A few fans with contemporary loops do exist, including a silver hall-marked one, and these were probably specially made to order for the lady to wear attached to a chatelaine. But we do not see them worn in this way in portraits, genre pieces or fashion prints of the time, although women with fans are frequently represented in such works of art. It is of special interest to see *how* they held their fans. It would appear, in the earlier part of the century, that the elegant way to hold a closed fan was between the third finger and the forefinger, somewhat in the manner of a cigarette, perhaps placing the thumb on the pivot end, thereby showing off to advantage a pretty, well-groomed hand (fig. 18b).

The correct way to handle a fan was part of etiquette and deportment. In the eighteenth century young ladies in well-to-do families received regular instruction in deportment from the dancing master, either at home or at dancing schools, and there was

32 *From Nivelon's instructions on deportment in* The Rudiments of Genteel Behaviour, *1737 — Plate III shows the positioning of the foot and describes the proper manner of walking with hands folded and a closed fan.*

also an abundance of literature which catered for this need. The English miss was instructed in the management and correct usage of her fan, being told that 'the fan is genteel and useful, therefore it is proper that young ladies should know how to make a genteel and proper use of it; in order that they may do so, I have pointed out to them six Positions of the Fan, genteel and very becoming'.[19]

The uses of the fan as a shield against a too hot fire, or to create a cooling wind, or to deter insects were understood, but unreasonable fluttering and twirling of it was considered absurd and affected. Notwithstanding it did give scope for a variety of expression, particularly in the hands of a practised exponent. It was this aspect of the fan which gave rise to humorous comments from the satirists of the day, and was the source of fanciful interpretations of the inner meaning of the language of the fan.

The language of the fan is a conceit which excites the imagination of many people, but it seems that the eighteenth-century allusions are not to be taken too seriously, and Joseph Addison's (1672-1719) article in the *Spectator* of 27 June, 1711 is purely satirical. The attitudes illustrated in the Dutch almanac, *De Nieuwe Princelyke Haagse Almanach Voor Het-Jaar, 1785,* –

33 *'The Lady with the Veil' (the artist's wife) by Alexandre Roslin (1718-93), c. 1768. Suzanne Roslin flirts with a fan. The fan guard is clearly carved, gilt and painted ivory, the fine sticks (monture squelette) pierced and gilt.*

'Céremonie', 'Congé, 'Ordinaire' and 'Conversation' — depict a genteel way of holding a fan on a specific occasion, and only go to show that it was not only the English Miss who knew the correct management of the fan; in fact, according to informed opinion in France, it was by the innumerable ways of handling a fan that 'one distinguishes the Princess from the Countess, and the Marchioness from the Commoner'.[20]

It is very probable that the code or codes known as the 'language of the fan' are a nineteenth-century invention, developed by the Parisian fan-maker J. Duvelleroy.

Forms of communication through the fan and with the fan did exist, but were more in the nature of a party game. A printed fan devised in 1797, by one Charles Badini gives a number of precise instructions. Several versions of this fan exist, the obverse and the reverse both inscribed. On one example in the Schreiber Collection[21] the top of the obverse is inscribed with the title of the leaf, 'Fanology or Speaking Fan', the object of which is set forth on a panel below in the following words:

The Telegraph of Cupid in this Fan
Though you should find suspect no wrong
'Tis but a simple and diverting Plan
for Ladies to Chit Chat and hold the Tongue.

On the left are given the 'Rudiments of Fanology', showing how conversation is to be carried on by signs and signals, and on the left is an 'Example'. Five small medallions with females in various attitudes are scattered over the leaf and lettered Signal 1, 2, 3, 4 and 5. To the left and right of the central female figures (Signal 5) are other medallions inscribed 'The Original Fanology or the Ladies' Conversation Fan

. . . Invented by Mr Chas. Francis Badini and Pubd. as the Act Directs by Proprietor Wm. Cock, No. 42 Pall Mall, August 7th 1797'. Below are the words 'Entered at Stationers' Hall'.

On the reverse are 'Examples', 'Questions' and 'Answers'. All versions of this fan are printed on paper, but some are known with plain wooden sticks while there are other elaborate composite sticks of wood, ivory and steel, etc. Evidently 'Fanology' was an amusing party game. Another publication appearing on 18 March 1797 and printed by Robert Clarke, shows a form of semaphore for the leisured person. In a similar vein were the messages on other printed fans of this period, such as the 'Fortune Telling Fan', the 'Casino Fan' (casino is a game of cards to which Casanova, among others, was much addicted), the 'Whist Fan' (' . . . If in doubt win the trick and be sure to KEEP YOUR TEMPER — Published for the benefit of Families and to prevent scolding'). This then is the 'business' of the fan, or, as the *Spectator* in 1711 so aptly declared: 'Women are armed with fans, as men are with swords'. Sometimes men too carried fans but it was exceptional and considered foppish — not a normal part of a gentleman's 'toilette'.[22]

Throughout the eighteenth century fans were, on all occasions, part of a woman's attire, and, as has been observed, no longer the prerogative of the very rich. That they reflect the social and political scene is but an indication that they had become an integral part of dress. Perhaps the best summing up is made by Hogarth in his satire entitled 'Evening' (1738) in which he indicates the character of the lustful shrewish wife by her fan, which shows Venus detaining Adonis from the Chase.

3
1800~1850

Dramatic changes seldom occur in the applied arts. Fans, at the turn of the eighteenth century, started to decrease in size, but while a smaller format which was more practical, easier to stow away into a reticule and more in keeping with the neater line of dress was evolving, the larger fans were still very much in evidence.

34 An Italian fan, c. 1805, an exquisite gift of the Grand Tour, with small ivory sticks and metal guards set with amethyst, other semi-precious stones and paste. The parchment leaf shows a view of the Colosseum painted in gouache with all the skill of the minaturist. The swan border and garlands and the engraved 'ler Janvier' on the guard suggest this fan could also have some French connections. (7¼ in. — 184 mm.)

It is possible that there were deeper causes behind these changes. The last decade of the eighteenth century witnessed the French Revolution and the revolutionary wars, with their repercussions and a general unrest throughout Europe. One of the results was that many trades, including fan-making, lost craftsmen and, even more significantly, apprentices, to the armies and navies of their respective countries. A few old masters may indeed have continued the long-standing traditional methods for very special objects, but a quicker and less labour-intensive specification was beginning to be needed for making cheaper and more numerous fans. The former aristocratic market no longer existed and new styles had crept in.

The materials which were available tended too to dictate shapes and design, and at this time the most readily available materials for carving ornaments such

48

as combs etc., were horn instead of expensive imported tortoiseshell, and bone instead of ivory.

An interesting new feature is the treatment of the pivot end of the fan. Instead of tapering to a 'snake head' shape, we now find most of these smaller fans with a little barrel-shaped end, the rivet often a neat,

circular, flat-cut steel sequin. There is little doubt that this fashion came from France: two fans exist commemorating the Peace of Amiens in 1802. One

35b A brisé fan, c. 1810. The sticks are of pierced ivory, painted with a central motif of a bunch of roses within a medallion, recalling earlier decorations; the golden guards are aglow with a miscellany of diamonds, peridots, amethysts, turquoises, jade, emeralds, cornelians etc., and a large rivet of mala- chite surrounded by rose diamonds is set at either side of the pivot. (6¾ in. – 170 mm.)

35a Detail from a painting of Marie Julie, wife of Joseph, one of Napoleon's brothers, by Robert Lefebre, signed and dated 1807. Her jewelled fan shows the influence set by the Empress Josephine at her coronation in 1804.

1 A fan leaf, painted in gouache, illustrating the marriage of Louis XIV, King of France, with Maria Theresa of Spain. The couple are seated in the centre beneath a canopy surrounded by ladies of the court, all with fans; a putto floats overhead holding a garland and branches of palm and olive, and on the right four other cupids are engaged in preparing the nuptial couch; this fan leaf has been removed from its mount and pasted on wood.

2 An early commemorative fan, dating from the first half of the eighteenth century, which suggests an important event, possibly the coronation of George II (1728) or, more probably, the marriage of his eldest daughter in 1734 to the Prince of Orange. Each of the ivory sticks bears a letter in silver piqué work, the sentence thus formed across the span reading 'THE ROYAL FAMILY'. The fine carving shows a royal crown in the centre, the lion and the unicorn in the reserves, and five portraits, probably of George II and some members of his family. The painted leaf has sustained some damage but shows Alexander and the family of Darius on the obverse, and Odysseus discovering Achilles among the daughters of Lycomedes on the reverse. (10¾ in. – 273mm.)

3,4 Two fans of the 1770s, commenting on the obsession of ladies of fashion for having their hair dressed in the high hairstyles.

3 Entitled 'La Folie des Dames de Paris'. The sticks and guards of this ivory fan are delicately carved and silvered. The single parchment leaf is painted with five vignettes on a Rococo background of floral motifs. The reverse

shows the ribs of the fan with painted medallions. (10¾ in. – 273mm.)

4 A carved and pierced ivory fan, the sticks and guards in typical Rococo style. The double painted paper leaf is burnished to give it a sheen and is of a type only found on French fans. The reverse is painted with a sketchy building set in a landscape. (10¾ in. – 273mm.)

of them is French and the other English, and, whereas the English fan still retains the characteristics of a late eighteenth-century fan, the French one is already smaller and terminates in the 'new' barrel end. Also, where there is a leaf, the proportion of the sticks to leaf has modified and the sticks are relatively tiny.

In 1816 the *Encyclopaedia Perenthis* or *Universal Dictionary of the Arts, Sciences, Literature, etc. (intended to supersede the use of other Books of Reference)*, printed in Edinburgh, describes, under the heading 'Fans – modern', the making of fans in very much the same way as did Diderot, in the *Encyclopédie*, some 50 years earlier. It is interesting to note that ' . . . the number of sticks rarely exceeds 22. The sticks are usually provided by the cabinet-makers or toy-men; the fan painters plait the papers, paint and mount them . . . ', confirming, albeit in less detail, the descriptions in the *Dictionnaire Méthodique*.

During the Empire (1804-15) a few very lavish fans were made, the guards encrusted with gems (fig. 35), to suit the tastes of the newly emerging aristocracy of ex-revolutionaries, the *nouveaux riches* who had survived into a new century. It is as though a new wave of thinking had set in, completely alien to the Baroque styles. There were no more Biblical subjects to be found and few figurative fans altogether; far more popular were those with gauze leaves embroidered with gold thread and spangles. The classical honeysuckle shape, the lyre, swags and medallions harmonize with the gowns of the period.

It may be because women were not so well educated in the classical sense (hardly surprising, when their formative years had been so unstable) that there are few fans with historical and mythological subjects. When they are found on fan leaves of this period, these subjects are usually printed and coloured in by hand.

Quantities of little horn, bone and ivory brisé fans with minimal painted decoration appeared on the market, small enough to fit into the indispensable reticule. The piercing is simple and patterns often repetitive and repeated, such as the honeysuckle motif which was prevalent in architectural decoration.

The manufacture of sticks and guards of fans in France was concentrated around Sainte Geneviève in the Oise,[1] and it would appear that the industry started to flourish there in the 1760s after the 'route nationale' came into being, which naturally facilitated communications with the capital where the fans were mounted and sold.

It is interesting to read that in 1792, during the Revolution, the craftsmen only worked on fan-making during the wintertime, working at the farms and in agriculture during the other seasons.

By the nineteenth century, whole families were employed in the making of sticks and guards, which included different operations, which were the specialities of different craftsmen. These included paring, piercing, turning (this was done on a special machine), gilding (usually reserved for the women), etc. For top-quality guards master sculptors all resided at Andeville. Materials used were sometimes indigenous, such as bone and horn, but mostly they were imported – ivory, fine English horn, tortoiseshell, mother-of-pearl and even wood. Messrs Smith in Ayrshire extolling the virtues of their 'fancy Scotchwood-work', proclaim in the *Art Journal* of 1850 that ' . . . among other things we have made large quantities of fans, ornamenting them in our own peculiar styles for the French market'.

One of the most important centres for carving ivory in France was the port of Dieppe which, during the Napoleonic wars, was a stronghold of the French Navy. Soldiers and sailors from around and about were, before conscription, if not actually making, then certainly familiar with the making of small objects such as combs, fans and fan sticks in which the region specialized. England possesses many examples of the work of French prisoners of war, such as the tiny working models of the guillotine carved in bone and ships with rigging and masts fabricated from materials which were at hand.

Records at Perth Prison (where the prisoners actually built the prison around themselves) state that they were given leave to make and sell their bone and horn wares at fairs and markets in the area. During the long winter evenings, with plentiful supplies of bone and horn from the farm animals, it may be assumed that fan sticks were among the objects they made and which they were permitted to sell at local fairs to help in their subsistence and to lessen the financial burden on their hosts.

It is no coincidence that the motifs on many little fairings in horn or imitation tortoiseshell in England at this period are typical of the patterns found on fine 'Dieppe' fans, such as the characteristic herringbone motif, and the ever-recurring honeysuckle design. Significant too is the fact that, a quarter of a century earlier, the *Dictionnaire Méthodique* mentions that it is to Rouen (a stone's throw from Dieppe) that the finest horn is imported from England. Not only did the French prisoners have the skills required, they were probably quite familiar with the materials they now found in England! The popular little brisé fan was an ideal vehicle for these skills, requiring no knowledge of painting and dispensing with the leaf

altogether.

At this period a fabric leaf came into vogue and it was in the pleating of the fan leaf that the eighteenth and nineteenth centuries differ most considerably. It has been seen that silk leaves became fashionable around the 1770s. It is not possible to treat fabric in the same way as paper or paper-like substances, or derivatives of leather which, by fixing onto a grooved wooden board and running a small coin shape along the grooves, could be scored into neat, regular pleats. Textiles cannot respond to this treatment, but a suitable method of folding them was devised by the end of the eighteenth century and was adopted systematically throughout the nineteenth and even into the twentieth century. This involved the use of paper moulds or presses which appear to have been made exclusively by the firm of Ducrot and Petit in Paris.[2]

Moulds were made of stout cardboard in varying sizes, to suit the differing proportions of fans. Basically they consisted of a double concertina of cardboard, folded in the middle and between which the painted or decorated fan leaf was placed. The mould was then firmly clamped into a tight-fitting cardboard sheath and the fan leaf left to 'set' in a warm atmosphere (fig. 37). Each sheath (of differing size) was marked with a number corresponding to the width of the pleat, which in turn corresponded with the number of sticks to be used (excluding the guards). Sticks were also numbered which allowed for easier mounting.

Measurements were all in 'pieds and pouces', the old French measurement of foot and thumb, the

36 *Five small brisé fans, all measuring approximately 6¼ in. (160 mm.), some of them with their own boxes. The closed fan on the bottom row on the left is of imitation tortoiseshell; above it is an open horn fan with a little painted floral garland. The white fan is of bone and its case, inscribed 'P.H.N., the gift of Fanny 29th June 1821', lies open beside it. Beneath are two more horn fans, the open one with its own cardboard case. The closed one shows well the flower-shaped cut steel rivet set into the characteristic barrel-shaped pivot of fans of this period. The uniformity of shape and patterns of the carvings are a study in themselves. c. 1815-20.*

'pouce' being the twelfth part of the 'pied' or 27 mm, the 'pied' measuring 3248 mm (which is slightly over one foot, or 12 in.).[3] This anachronistic form of measurement continued into the twentieth century and, indeed, until fans ceased to be made in France.[4]

The fashion magazines of the time give a vivid idea of how and where fans could be used. In 1808 *La Belle Assemblée* stated that 'No lady of fashion appears in public without a reticule — which contains her handkerchief, fan, card money and essence bottle'. A cross section of random notes appended to the 'toilettes' in the fashion magazines shows that by 1815 fans were small and relatively uncomplicated. Ackerman's *Repository of Arts*, noted in March 1817 that: 'Fans have rather decreased in size lately; white

37 The fan mould, showing the two identical
accordion-pleated cards between which the painted
fabric leaf was placed. It is seen here with the sheath
marked No. 96, 16 Brins, 12 Pouces; and the standard
fan-maker's ruler.

crape fans richly embroidered in silver are most fashionable at present.' On 1 October 1817, in *London Fashions* the accompanying description of a plate showing an evening dress reads: ' . . . white kid gloves and spangled crape fan'. After the death of Princess Charlotte (November 1817) the whole nation went into mourning, and in December 1817 Ackerman notes, again in *London Fashions*: ' . . . plain black crape fans, black shamoy gloves and black shoes . . . '. By May 1818 though, it is back to a 'small ivory fan' as accessory to a 'Dinner dress', and for an evening dress ' . . . hair arranged in a few light ringlets on each temple, small ivory fan.'

At this stage it does seem that fans were worn mostly in the evening, on formal or semi-formal occasions, and that the small bone and ivory fans were

used as dance-fans for marking one's partner's name for the cotillion or country dance. No doubt it is to one of these that Jane Austen refers in *Mansfield Park* when William 'works away at his partner's fan'. Another of Miss Austen's heroines, Catherine, in *Northanger Abbey*, at a public reception at Bath, endeavours to conceal herself from the attentions of John Thorpe: 'that she might not appear to observe or expect him, she kept her eyes intently fixed on her fan'.

Although 'puzzle' fans were known in the previous century, they now make a new appearance, which Eudocia, the fashion gossip of *Ackerman's Repository*, describes as a novelty from Paris in the New Year of 1819:

I had almost forgot to mention to you a new fashion, and one which is eagerly adopted. I mean 'les éventails à surprise', which aught rather to be called changeable fans. They are composed of crape, which is cut to resemble lace, and spangled: in the middle of the fan is a small picture, which may be varied so as to show four subjects, two on each side. These toys afford a pretty Frenchwoman an opportunity, which she knows how to use, to display all her graces to the utmost advantage. The play of her countenance, the easy eloquence of her motion, the many pretty things she has to say on each of the different subjects which the fan presents, all combine to render her for the moment an attractive, and even dangerous, object to a susceptible heart. But these changeable fans, and my eternal habit of digressing, have scarcely left me room to tell you that the colours most in fashion are celestial blue, slate-colour, deep rose-colour, fawn and 'ponceau'. Nothing, however, is more fashionable than white . . . .

The reference to colours is interesting. On the whole the colour of the fan contrasted with the outfit, and it is not until 1858 that the *Ladies Treasury* decrees that: 'Our fair readers must observe that to be quite à la mode, their fans must [in colour] correspond with their dresses.'

In 1822 and 1823 fans were still small, often made of ivory or mother-of-pearl by Eastern craftsmen, and to the fashionable small format, but by the 1830s they had grown and could no longer fit into the

---

38 'Full Dress', a fashion plate from The Lady's Monthly Museum, *June 1807, showing a cockade fan with spy-glass in the pivot in use.*

39 Three cockade fans c. 1808-12. From left to right: an ivory cockade probably made for export in the East; a horn cockade with applied gold leaf and silver and some steel spangles containing a spy-glass in the barrel-shaped pivot; a paper-fine light horn cockade pierced and painted with a garland of flowers.

smaller reticules which 'cannot contain more than a purse and a fine cambric handkerchief'. Evening dresses and ball dresses described in the *Ladies' Museum* of 1830 were accompanied by a 'cedar fan

richly ornamented with gold', and a ball dress of 'gaze d'Ispahan' was worn with a 'carved cedar fan'. In the same year the feather fan made an appearance.

Townsend's Monthly Selection of Parisian Costume shows Paris leading the fashions with London not averse to following them and fans are no longer used only on formal occasions. In May 1832 it notes that:

Ladies carry large fans, both in the promenades and in the evening: they are called éventails Chinois [Chinese fans]; they are made exactly like those that come from China. The sticks are japanned, and the fan is a skin, upon which are appliqué small objects in ivory and mother-of-pearl. The coloured pearl called burgos is employed for the dresses, the figures and views are in ivory. Sometimes the object is a bird, the wings of which are made of feathers carefully appliqué [stuck on].

This description tallies closely with the composition of the Canton, or Mandarin fan, which was exported throughout the nineteenth century in its distinctive lacquer box with a painted lined interior in silk (fig. 65).

This popular export fan was made in China specifically for the European market. It was composed of a leaf of fabric or paper lavishly decorated on both sides, the obverse usually bearing an oriental court scene with numerous figures, their hands and faces of applied ivory, their clothes of appliqué silk material. The reverse might have a similar scene, but birds, butterflies and flowers could be depicted, and some particularly elegant fans bear a detailed and minutely executed seascape, usually showing a trading harbour. The sticks could be quite plain or highly ornamental, and varied from lacquer (black, red or even green and sometimes a combination of all three), to ivory (pierced and carved), cloisonné on filigree silver or gilded metal, wood and, very seldom, bone. The later ones were often furnished with silk tassels which hung on jade or rose quartz beads.

In June 1832 *Townsend's* reports that 'Some ladies carry enormous Chinese fans instead of parasols'. The following year seems to have been profitable to the fan industry as fans were ' . . . seen in all the most elegant salons. It is the fashion to place a variety on the consoles, tables, etc., which are offered to visitors the same as screens are in Winter, they are very desirable in this warm season.' In September the 'Chinese fans of Japan or ivory of an enormous size, are an indispensable part of the toilette or even demi-toilette'; while in October 'Fans continue to be used both at the theatres and in the saloons, those with Chinese and Indian designs have the preference'. In the earlier part of 1833 it is noted that the most admired fans were of tortoiseshell inlaid with gold.

It can be inferred that a great variety of shapes and sizes were back in vogue, from the circular cockade, made on the principle of a brisé fan and sometimes containing a little spy glass in the pivot (which is the centre of the cockade) (fig. 39), to fabric and feather fans, with every variation in between.

From about 1815 onwards the fan became more colourful, and fan leaves with printed or painted pictures, or both, were fashionable. Some detailed

40 Ivory and mother-of-pearl fan, the guards decorated with a chequered design of inlay, the sticks having the characteristic perforations and overall motifs of design which are associated with the factories of Ste Geneviève in the Oise. The printed leaf is hand-coloured, the central part depicting a couple visiting a family in a park. It is a charming vignette of polite society in the 1830s clearly showing the dress of both men and women and even the child's clothes. c. 1830.

41 *A French ivory fan, the sticks and guards heavily decorated and gilt with eighteenth-century type motifs. The paper leaf is chromolithograph representing a scene in a park within a border of ornate gold fronds. The figures wear a fairly accurate representation of seventeenth-century (early Louis XIV) costume in keeping with the current nostalgia for earlier times. c. 1845.*

little scenes appear on the leaves of printed fans in the 1830s, brilliantly coloured in by hand, accurately portraying polite society in the dress which characterized it (fig. 40). These prints, and other cheaper ones destined for the less expensive theatrical fans, were printed in France and bear a serial number which is identifiable at the deposits of the Bibliothèque Nationale in Paris. Quantities of these fans were exported to Spain, and often bear captions in Spanish. Not so very far back in time, during the Peninsula Wars, England too had exported printed fan leaves to Spain.

The sticks of these printed fans of the Romantic era were relatively simple, but the guards were often elaborate, containing gem stones with a predominance of semi-precious stones such as coral, turquoise and amethyst.

If she did not exactly create a new fashion in fans, the Duchesse de Berri certainly indulged in fancy dress balls[6] and a decade or so later they were still popular. Happy hours could be spent in planning a costume, and historical accuracy was sought right along the line. This passion for historical period pieces swept over Europe, and at every level, from Violet le Duc's work on the systematic classification and restoration of buildings, to his book on costume. The hand fixed feather fans with a mirror in the centre, to be worn with imitation period or theatrical dress, are an expression of this obsession for bygone times.

This nostalgia was reflected in the decoration of fans and fan leaves, with the curious result that one can sometimes find a fan with a chromo-lithograph or a print coloured in gouache or plain water colours of a seventeeth-century scene, on sticks carved and pierced to imitate the eighteenth-century style, with a chased metal loop in the rivet which is purely nine-teenth-century. (fig. 41)

In richness of appearance some of the better carved fans rival those of the eighteenth century, and the techniques of printing had developed to permit a much greater variety of effect. The paper which was employed for fans of this quality was usually brightly coloured and embossed, often with gold, adding to the general effect of luxury.

On the principle that imitation is the sincerest form of flattery, these fans featured what people most admired, and there is no pretence at deception, for it is not uncommon to find fans the obverse of which are decorated with figures in Renaissance costume, while the reverse show scenes with people in contemporary attire.

In 1842, Queen Victoria gave a munificent costume ball at Buckingham Palace. The queen appeared as Queen Philippa while Prince Albert wore a costume modelled on that of Edward III. Planché, who compiled a book recording every noteworthy dress worn by the court dignitaries, mentions that minute care was taken to ensure complete accuracy; the only deviation which the Queen (still young and attractive) allowed herself was to omit the sleeves of her heraldic costume. An ivory brisé fan commemorates the event, and the artist has used Planché's colourful plates to copy 30 little medallions, each showing one of the protagonists and captioning their role. It is not known whether this was a royal gift, for, like Queen Elizabeth I, Queen Victoria was the recipient and the donor of many a fan, with the difference that some of hers are now preserved in the Museum of London. Many of them reflect their owner's taste, and, by inference, her personailty: not all are the valuable

During the Restoration of the French monarchy (1814-1830), the young and fashion conscious Duchesse de Berri (Marie Caroline de Bourbon (1798-1870)) gave a costume ball at which participants were invited to wear the dress of the court of Louis XV.[5] Prints and pictures of that period were studied in detail and a search made throughout Paris of fans resembling those of the eighteenth century. Finally an old stock was discovered and bought up, and again, legend would have it, this lead, overnight, to a revival of the fan as an indispensable accessory — hardly a very credible story. It does, however, lead one to suppose that second-hand fans were acceptable accessories, and did not have the adverse connotation of being 'old fashioned', which in a new materialistic society was attached to out-of-date hats and other articles of clothing.

presentation pieces which she holds in the royal portraits, such as the one the Queen was pleased to accept from the Fan Makers' Company as a souvenir of the Fan Exhibition of 1897, of which she was the patroness. Two of them have views of her residences; one of Balmoral (colour plate 5) is a well-painted silk leaf, with sprigs of fern and heather framing a romantic view of the castle she loved; it is signed S.E. Sydney. Another fan, signed Cte Nils, has a view of Windsor painted on its silk leaf.

Queen Victoria's attachment to her family and home life is also embodied in an endearing fan which is quite patently the work of an amateur painter, the leaf decorated with fronds of seaweeds and shells and the reverse set with photographs of Princess Christian's children.

Home-made or otherwise, fans were very much a part of the royal fashion scene. In 1871, *The Queen* published an engraving of a most competent fan designed and painted by HRH the Princess Louise (September 1871, p. 150), showing a winter scene with skaters on a lake. The ladies wear short skirts and the fashionable small, forward-tilted hats, and it is evident that Queen Victoria's talents as an artist were inherited by at least one of her daughters.

Accounts of fans as royal wedding gifts abound. From 1881 there is a description of a wedding present to Princess Victoria of Baden from the Crown Princess of Prussia (another of Queen Victoria's daughters), which was a replica of a fan given to Princess Louisa 25 years earlier; it was mounted on ivory and gold with the name Victoria in rubies on the guard, painted by Emil Doepler the Younger and mounted by the jeweller Schaper of Berlin. Not quite so spectacular, but nevertheless mentioned, were the lace fan presented by Baroness Erlanger to Princess Louise of Schleswig Holstein, and another designed and painted for her by a Miss Loch. In 1894 Lilly Reuss, of Carlton Studio, Manchester, designed and painted a fan for the then Duchess of York with a number of significant decorative motifs such as a heart framed in York roses.

All these fans make royalty appear quite accessible, and queens and princesses could, just like any other clever lady, put a fine piece of work to advantage. In June 1895 the Duchess of York purchased a fan leaf at an amateur exhibition. It was designed and painted by a Miss Crabb, and the central vignette was derived from Reynolds painting of the Ladies Waldegrave. In July of that year, the same leaf was mounted on richly carved mother-of-pearl sticks with the initial H and a coronet in diamonds on the guard, by Duvelleroy, and presented to the Princess Hélène d'Orleans on the occasion of her marriage, by HRH the Duchess of Teck (who was the mother of the Duchess of York)!

4

1851-1900

The state of the mid-nineteenth-century fan industry was recorded in the catalogue and jury reports of the International Exhibition of 1851, a memorable date, marking the opening of the first of a veritable 'rash' of international exhibitions which were to crop up all over the world throughout the remainder of the nineteenth and into the twentieth century.

42 *A typical high Victorian fan, with heavily decorated mother-of-pearl sticks and guards, carved, pierced and much gilded, with a pretence of a paper leaf almost like a woven ribbon, printed and painted with ladies and gentlemen in 'eighteenth-century' dress. c. 1856.*

One of the most notable makers was Duvelleroy in Paris, and a collection of fans from his establishment caused comment and much admiration, and won the prize in its class. The *Art Journal* (1851) states that he is:

at the present moment so entirely without rival in his trade that no lady's 'corbeille de mariage' is considered complete without one of Mr Duvelleroy's fans. Some of them are indeed perfect bijoux, and are decorated with a profusion of expensive ornament which render them objects of the greatest luxury. Besides being studded with precious stones, the most eminent artists of Paris do not scruple to make some of their most finished designs upon them. Roqueplan, Johannot, Gavarni,

43 Mme Moitessier by Jean A. Dominique Ingres
(1780-1867), 1856. A Junoesque lady, her hand
reposes on a half-closed fan, its small leaf and heavy
rounded shoulders very much in keeping with the
fashionable shapes reflected in the painting.

44 *A magnificent fan by Alexandre, signed and dated 1869, with ivory sticks carved by Brisevin and painted with vignettes representing scenes of the Henri III period, supporting a beautiful leaf of cream lace. (11⅛ in. – 280 mm.)*

Eugène Lami and Dupré have from time to time been employed to enhance their attractions.

At the Paris Exhibition of 1868, it was to Mr Alexandre of Paris that the highest honours were awarded, a firm with an already well-established reputation, with shops throughout Europe and in America, and certainly enjoying royal patronage which included the Queen of Spain, the French Empress Eugénie, the Empress of Russia and others.

It was without doubt the French fan which was most highly esteemed, and it was exported all over the Western world. One of France's most important markets was America, and statistics show a significant drop in overseas sales of fans at the time of the Civil War.[1] By 1867 the Civil War in America was concluded and the following year marked the date of the International Exhibition in Paris which attracted many American businessmen and merchants. *Harpers Bazaar*, 'a repository of Fashion, Pleasure and Instruction' (note the order!), made its entrance of 2 November 1867 and relates that the wives and daughters who accompanied the American visitors returned with trunks filled with French treasures for their wardrobes — and the sales statistics of fans in France for that year had risen considerably. From then on there is a steady rise in sales, the best period being between 1871 and 1890 with a good revival between 1894 and 1904.[2]

A mechanical cutter (a machine to facilitate the fretwork on fan sticks) was invented in 1859[3] by Alphonse Baud, thus speeding up the manufacture of fans and allowing prices to compare favourably with the imported items from China and Japan.

The second half of the nineteenth century was one of the most prolific times for the use and manufacture of fans, and, thanks to developments in communications in a rapidly shrinking world and to the many International Exhibitions, they become a significant part of the social scene.

London set the scene in Paxton's Crystal Palace in 1851, followed by exhibitions in 1862, 1871-4 and 1925. Paris held Expositions in 1855, 1867, 1878, 1889, 1900, 1937 and there were others in Lyon in 1873, Vienna in 1873, Philadelphia in 1876, Sydney in 1879, Melbourne in 1880, Amsterdam in 1883, Antwerp in 1885 and 1930, New Orleans in 1885-6, Barcelona in 1888 and 1929, Copenhagen in 1888, Brussels in 1888, 1897, 1910 and 1935, Chicago in 1893 and 1933, St Louis in 1904, Liège in 1905 and 1930, Milan in 1906, Turin in 1911, Gand in 1913, New York and San Francisco in 1939.

Not only were fans exhibited by many countries on these occasions, but in nearly every case there was also a commemorative fan issued for the exhibition,

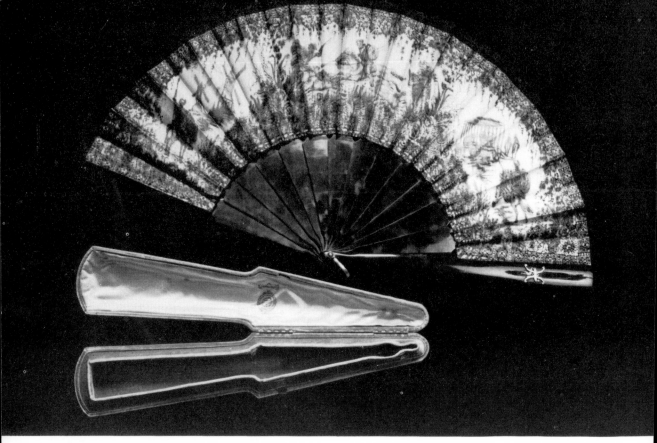

and sometimes more than one, a hand-out from one or other of the exhibition pavilions or stands.

On 1 May 1878, the President of the French Republic, Maréchal de Mac-Mahon, Duke of Magenta, opened the Universal Paris Exposition in the presence of, among the throng of Royalty and potentates, the Prince of Wales and the Lord Mayor of London.[4] This was a resurrection for France, after a civil war and crushing defeat only six years before! Some of the streets had not been made up and it was necessary to cross the Seine to get from one part of the Exhibition grounds to the other. The *Ladies' Treasury* is practical and prepares its readers contemplating a visit to Paris for all eventualities; it advises 'Comfortable footwear and for fine weather a complete linen costume then, is the best thing, with umbrella and fan hanging to your belt'. Most fans, at this time, were furnished with a loop, and they could be worn as directed in the magazine just quoted, or hanging from a loop in a ribbon at the wrist.

It could be that the English ladies at the Paris Exhibition wore silk fans of the type illustrated in the *Englishwoman's Domestic Magazine* of 1874. This 'pretty ornament' was intended to be worn at the waistband, to which it fastened by means of a bronze

hook and from which it hung down in the shape of a 'dainty little dagger'. The fan itself was of the cockade or half-cockade type, and an identical illustration of it appears in *La Mode Illustrée, Journal de la Famille*, also in 1874, as a Modèle from Mme Leconte, Rue du Quatre Septembre 31.

Lace fans were becoming increasingly popular. Already in the previous decade they had won gold medals in their class at the Exhibition of 1862 (fig. 45), and the industry had been greatly encouraged in their respective countries by both the Empress Eugénie and Queen Victoria, who appreciated its quality the more because of her family connections with Belgium.[5] Ireland and Devon were the centres in Great Britain renowned for this art, and when in 1885 Queen Victoria gave her daughter Princess Beatrice a fan (among other gifts) on the occasion of her marriage to Prince Henry of Battenburg, with a view of Osborne painted on it, the ladies of Waterford in Ireland also gave a fan, made of the finest Cappoquin point lace, mounted on mother-of-pearl. (The lace was made by the poor girls in Miss Keane's school at Cappoquin on the Blackwater.)[6] A fan leaf made entirely of lace poses technical difficulties in the making, since lace is usually worked in flat strips, and the circular shape of a fan leaf requires of the maker special skills and experience.

Black and white lace fans were both used, the black ones not only for mourning but for evening wear and the theatre, while the white ones made eminently acceptable gifts. Because of the skills required in their making, they could be very expensive, and La Mode Illustrée advises its readers to make their own lace, giving full instructions for the stitches to be used (an imitation of the point d'Alençon was devised) and it goes on to indicate how the fan leaves thus made should be backed with silk crêpe and should be mounted onto readymade ivory or carved wooden sticks.

The art of making and decorating fans by the gifted dilettante was rapidly taking on. To begin with brisé fans were used for this purpose, usually wooden ones upon which it was easy to draw and then colour; (fig. 46); ivory was also available for the more ambitious amateur. The Queen gives numerous hints and patterns over the years for decorating fans, whether it be with stippled ferns or other naturalistic subjects, or with the very popular monograms and crests which were bought on sheets of paper, cut out and applied to blades of fans (fig. 47). Strong gum Arabic or diamond cement was recommended for fixing them, and they were usually placed on one side only of the fan, the largest and most showy at the top, decreasing in size as they went down.

By 1887, Hugh Rowley in Brighton[7] was instructing in painting on skin, silk, etc., all to be purchased from Duvelleroy, and fans decorated with love and care were often offered as Christmas gifts or even wedding presents. The Journal des Goncourt mentions Princess Matilde, cousin of Napoleon III, indulging in this pastime, and one of her signed fans is preserved in the Musée Carnavalet in Paris.

In his comprehensive book entitled L'Art de Peindre et de composer les Eventails, etc. G. Fraipont warns against the enthusiastic mama wanting her daughter to 'do something genteel and lady-like such as painting fans', in a witty paragraph reminiscent of

Noel Coward's song: 'Don't put your daughter on the stage . . . '. Clearly there were abuses but fortunately many of the horrors have perished.

Also popular were feather fans and, in 1876, the Englishwoman's Annual, describing some 'homemade' gifts for Christmas, declares that 'for a lady, a fan is always a graceful and acceptable gift, and those with feather ornamentation are the great favourites for the time being' — a time which would continue into the twentieth century, depriving many birds of their plumage and endangering more than one species.

The feather industry achieved vast proportions in the nineteenth century, affording employment for large numbers of skilled and unskilled workpeople, and, by 1913, 50,000 were alleged to be employed in France alone.[8]

An earlier mention has been made of feather fans in the 1830s, and the influence of colonization of far away countries by Europe cannot, in this context, be underestimated. Feathers, in whatever form, are by their very nature a symbol of display (as in the Red Indian headdress). Furthermore all the international exhibitions would have brought to notice ethnographical fans, many of which were made of feathers.

In 1858 The Ladies' Treasury gives a history of the fan and concludes: ' . . . nowadays they are again expanding, and the graceful feather fan is seen in the hand of beauty.' Ostrich feathers are perhaps those most readily associated with fans and they were used for this purpose as early as the 1870s. Initially the black and white feathers of the male bird were used, but later the brown feathers of the female made elegant, if more restrained, fans.

Centres for the rearing and farming of ostriches grew up, but never so systematically or as successfully as in the Cape Province of South Africa.[9] In 1881 there were sales six times a year at public auction in sales rooms in Mincing Lane (London) and from the annual statement of trade and shipping of the Union of South Africa it may be seen that the sale of ostrich feathers was one of considerable value. On 18 May 1881, the revenue in pounds sterling was:

Great Britain	1,931,575
Canada	3,868
Austria	3,717
Belgium	365
France	20,303
Germany	22,289
USA	288,806

This set of figures is of interest in enabling one to draw a number of conclusions. The tiny proportion of sales to Belgium, for example, must prove two

46   A wooden brisé fan, hand-painted and decorated in tones of greys and black, inscribed on the left guard 'The Lady James Murray, from Colonel H. Hope Crealock 1st Sept. 1868. Eastwood'. On the reverse the letter M is painted in flowers and ribbons on a lilac-coloured ground which leads one to suppose that the lady was a widow observing half-mourning: a very competent example of a 'do-it-yourself' gift. (9⅛ in. – 230 mm.)

47   An ivory brisé fan with carved guardsticks, ornamented with embossed crests – regimental, personal etc. The decoration is carefully carried out according to instructions to be found in the ladies' magazines of the period, with the larger designs at the top, the smaller ones tapering into the narrower base of the sticks. c. 1870. (9⅛ in. – 230 mm.)

48 *Too Early, by James Tissot (1836-1902), c.1874.*
Dressed for the party, complete with their 'frou-frou'
of frills and bows, the ladies make ample use of their
fans, the large striped one as much in fashion at that
time as the smaller one deployed by the lady in white
on the far right.

things: that by now Belgium was getting most of her
ostrich feathers from the Congo or her other colonies,
and that, in the second place, ostrich feather fans
were perhaps not so popular as elsewhere — the
obvious reason for this being the excellency of the
top quality lace still being made throughout the
country, and constituting at this time an important
luxury export.

It may be inferred too that Austria, with its great
Empire, was using feathers from birds hunted within
its own vast territories, such as the eagle and the
pheasant. The ladies accompanying fashionable shoot-
ing parties were presented with boxfuls of feathers
from the shot birds, for use in ornamenting hats,
muffs and fans, in just the same way that the fox's
brush is the prize of the ladies at the Hunt. Big birds

and little birds from all over the world served the
fashionable woman, from the tiny stuffed humming
bird perched within the centre of a circular feather
fan from Rio de Janeiro (fig. 49), to the half wing
of the proud Austrian eagle, mounted on tortoiseshell
with the lady's initials in gold or diamonds in the
guard (fig. 50).

In order to earn the extra penny, women would
take in ostrich feathers and fans for recurling, an
operation which was carried out at home over a
steaming kettle with a small knife-like instrument.[10]

In the 1870s fans were getting bigger until, in the
1880s, they had achieved truly monstrous proportions. In that typical 'chatty' style, *The Queen*
describes the fans of the day:

By the way, alluding to the Opera, I must not omit
to mention that the small pocket fans, made either
of ivory or tortoiseshell, which were recently so
popular, are now succeeded by immense fans,
made of either silk or satin embellished with
paintings and trimmed with lace. These fans are
called Corisande. They are specially popular in
black and white; the flowers are scattered and not

painted in a wreath. The black fans mounted with either tortoiseshell or ebony sticks are very appropriate for demi-toilettes. A tuft of roses, a bunch of lilac, and a branch of thorn with red berries produces a charming effect painted on both black and white silk fans.

In the 1880s both silk and fine gauze were used for bigger and bigger fans, hilariously commented on by the humourists (figs. 54, 55), and hardly a week went by without some reference to fans in the women's magazines.

By 1870, the industry of fan-making was well established in most countries on the Continent of Europe, and was being promoted to a considerable degree in England. *The Queen* (23 July, 1870), advo-

cates fan-making as an employment for women, and goes on to mention a forthcoming exhibition of fans from all countries brought together at the South Kensington Museum (now the Victoria and Albert Museum) to further the interest in the subject. There is also mention of a competition which would be included in the international exhibition to take place in the Salons lists signed fan leaves. Among them herself. Prices are quoted too, and they could vary from a penny to £200 or £300 — but these high prices were mostly consistent with the leaf being decorated by a well-known artist.

Fan painting had pretensions to being an art form, and many well-known painters whose names appear in the Salons lists signed fan leaves. Among them Philippe Rousseau, Veysserat, Vibert, Diaz, Glaize, Eugène Lami, Rosa Bonheur, Calamatta, Boutry,

49 Two feather fans from South America, c. 1870, on turned ivory handles, one with its own box with the maker's label: Louisa Bittancourt, Florista, Rio de Janeiro; the one on the right is adorned with a stuffed humming bird and bright green beetle wings.

50 A fashion page from The Queen for 5 May 1894, ▷ showing a ball gown, 'the Orchid', in mauve satin, a perfect foil for the eagle feather fan with tortoiseshell sticks and guards which is illustrated with it.

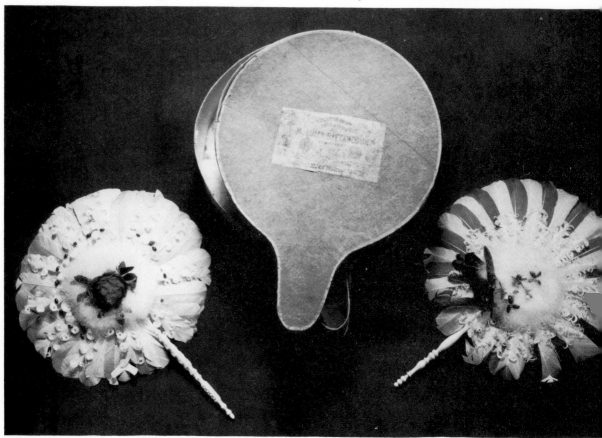

51 An asymmetrical goose feather fan on blond
tortoiseshell sticks, the guard bearing the initials
'D.R.' in diamonds – a fitting gift for Mrs James A.
de Rothschild on her marriage in 1913. (19½ in. –
495 mm. at its longest point)

Chaplin, Corot, Gavarni, Depenne, Armand Dumarecq, Ferrogi, all painted leaves which were made up by the Maison Duvelleroy. Some noteworthy painters actually specialized in fan-painting: outstanding among them was the Australian Ch. Conder (who spent many years in Paris); other well known artists were M. Soldé, Donzel (father and son), Cécile Chenevière, Sailly, Lazellas, Ostolle and Van Garden.

Although Fraipont expounds assiduously on composition, colour and all the techniques of painting fans and many fashionable artists painted and signed them, yet it is not widely known that painters such as Degas, Gauguin and Lautrec were the authors of many a fan leaf. Their interest was one of style and composition and they do not appear to have been concerned with the fashion aspect of the subject.

The Pre-Raphaelites in England concerned themselves with fans and, in 1867, Holman Hunt painted a fly on the fan of his enamorata. It was her 21st birthday and he was alluding to this 'fly in the ointment' of their future happiness, the cursed Table of Affinities which prevented their marriage, she being his deceased wife's sister.[11]

With the opening of Japan to the West,[12] there was a renewed and ever-growing interest in the Orient, and the influence of the Japanese prints which flooded the markets was felt in the changing artistic world. In fact all the artistic manifestations of the time found an expression, either on the leaves of fans or in their shape and composition. The Pre-Raphaelites certainly painted fans, as did the French Impressionists, and photography which was establishing itself as an alternative to portraiture had an indirect influence on fans. Indeed, some fans are covered with the popular *cartes de visite*, and there are series which were issued with a collection of photographic portraits of the royal family, music hall artists, opera singers and others.

The Aesthetic Movement did much to promote the eastern influence, the great exponent of this being Liberty, where fans from the East and objects with fan motifs could be purchased. In the 1880s Kate Greenaway ladies and children romp on the leaves of fans while more conventional floral motifs still decorate the large gauze and satin mounts. The cartoonist Du Maurier always represents the conventional hostess complete with her large fan, while the 'yallery greenery' lady droops over a peacock feather contraption — probably a Liberty import from India.

It was at the end of the nineteenth century that the big department stores emerged, and how and where fans were purchased is yet another aspect of their place in the social pattern; it is apparent that

70

52

53

◁ 52 A dark tortoiseshell fan c. 1885, with gold initials applied to the guard. The black silk leaf is
painted with pink and cream roses and is signed
F. Gardon.

53 Portrait of Adelaide Marie, Countess of Iveagh
by George Elgar Hicks, signed and dated 1885-94.
A dark fan was the fashionable accessory to complement a dress of light tone at this period, and the
touches of colour on the painted leaf were often
picked out cunningly to match ribbons or piping; in
this case the pinks of the roses match the sash.

54, 55 Caricatures from Punch lampooning the size
and texture of fans in the 1880s.

54 From Punch 1882, by Harry Furness.

55 Beware of Those Treacherous Gauze Fans;
Society picture from Punch 1887, by G. du Maurier.

STALLS.
54

TIME PRESENT—FAN DEVELOPMENT.

A CAUTION TO LADIES.

(Beware of those Treacherous Gauze Fans.)

1887.

Sir Pompey Bedell. "WELL—A—NOW THAT I HAVE THOROUGHLY EXPLAINED TO YOU WHAT MY CONVICTIONS ARE WITH REGARD
TO THE IRISH QUESTION, I WILL PROCEED TO——BUT—A—I AM REALLY ALMOST AFRAID I BEGIN TO PERCEIVE—A—THAT MY VIEWS
ON THE SUBJECT FAIL TO AROUSE YOUR INTEREST, MISS MASHAM!"

55

now, more than at any other time, fans were regarded as fashion accessories in the same light as gloves and 'novelties'.

The specialized fan houses were wholesaling to the larger shops, so that the product of the most important fan houses such as Duvelleroy, Kees or Lachelin could be obtained from La Maison de Blanc in Paris, or Harrods and Liberty in London.

All these influences led to a peak in the interest in fans in the 1890s, resulting in the Karlsruhe Exhibition of 1891,[13] specifically devoted to fans, modern and ancient and ethnographical. In England the Worshipful Company of Fan Makers held an Exhibition at Drapers' Hall in London in May 1890.

New shapes emerged as a desire for novelty and to break with the traditional became more pronounced; Frederick Penberthy, for example, won a prize for a

56 *Two of the larger 1880s fans showing the transparency of the gauze leaf. Left: plain ivory sticks and guards; the creamy gauze leaf of this fan is painted with birds and applied with machine-made lace; it still retains its silk loop and tassel. (14 in. — 355 mm.) Right: a more modest wooden fan painted to simulate bone or ivory; the gauze leaf with its tiny sprigs of flowers, birds and insects is threaded in neat rows with ivory satin ribbon. (13¾ in. — 350 mm.)*

5 A memento from a Highland visit figures on this smoky mother-of-pearl fan, the initials V.R. beneath an applied royal crown in one of the guards proclaiming its ownership by Queen Victoria. A view of Balmoral is hand-painted on the silk leaf, with the purple hills in the background, framed with sprays of heather and ferns (signed S.E. Sydney). *c.* 1860. (10¾ in. – 273mm.)

6 A souvenir of a first ball in 1862, this shaped fan is made on the principle of a brisé fan from 'petals' of stiffened silk. It was a type of fan which was popular for over a decade, and this one is decorated with a bunch of artificial moss roses in the right-hand guard. It comes with its own box; the label inside the lid is inscribed 'Sold by J.W. Sherriff, 11. Ludgate Street, London'. (9½ in. – 236mm.)

7 A mother-of-pearl fan, the sticks and guards embellished with gold scrollwork and the leaf of exquisitely worked lace, with two amorini supporting a crown and cypher in the centre. This fan was a gift to the Princess May of Teck (later Queen Mary) from the laceworkers of Honiton and others on the occasion of her wedding in 1893. (12¾ in. – 321 mm.)

8 An amber fan, the arched silk leaf decorated with the popular iris motif and signed by I. Gerard. The reverse is painted with the crown and cypher of Princess Helena Victoria, and the fan is complete with its own Paris Duvelleroy box. c. 1900. (8¼ in. – 210mm to the top of the guard.)

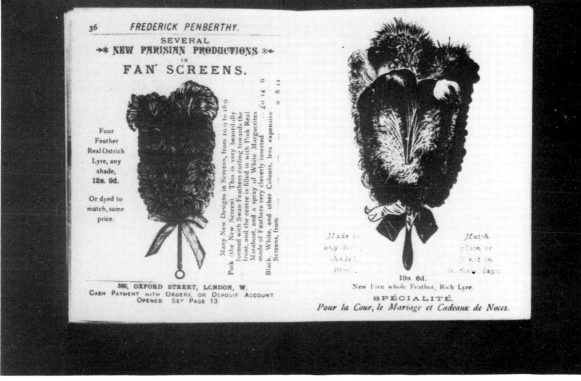

57 *Advertisement from F. Penberthy's catalogue,*
1890.

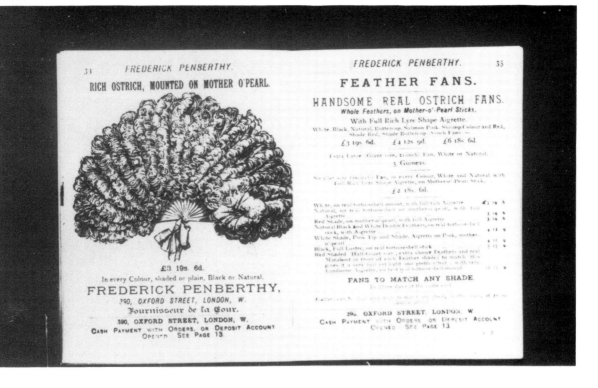

feather fan inspired by a combination of the Elizabethan and Prince of Wales' feather shapes, and a butterfly fan, fitted with a mechanical device to open and close its immense wings also went on display. If it was highly impractical (it was patented), it nevertheless set a trend for large gauze fan leaves being cut out to form a butterfly wing, or, a few years later, a bird or an animal, or the petal of a flower, and, if some of the critics of the Exhibition complained of a lack of good design, they were looking backward, rather than in advance to the shape of things to come.

Mention must be made here of the great fan collections which were formed towards the turn of the century. Princess May of Teck, later Queen Mary, was presented with many a fine fan (colour plate 7), and then formed an important royal collection at approximately the same time as Queen Margherita of Italy.[14] Large and small collections were made, often through the good offices of the special distributors of fans such as Duvelleroy, where clients were advised on the purchase of both new and antique fans. They also undertook repairs, and some cannibalization of old fans took place. But it was not uncommon for a lady actually to use a fine eighteenth-century fan, the stigma of the second-hand never touching on the fan!

As the century drew to a close, every type of fan was in use, from the great feather fans which were to become part of Court uniform, to the little imitation 'Directoire' fans, a-glitter with sequins, and no capital city was without an establishment of renown; Paris boasted Duvelleroy, Kees, Hoguet and others. In England, where earlier in the century fans could only be purchased from shops which sold other goods, such as Rimmel's perfumery, there were now fan shops in most of the major cities, and in London many of the fashionable thoroughfares could claim at least one fan boutique besides the sections devoted to fans in the big department stores. One should also cite Bach in Madrid, Rodek in Vienna, Paul Telge the jeweller in Berlin, the fabled Fabergé in St Petersburg and Tiffany in New York, to name but a few.

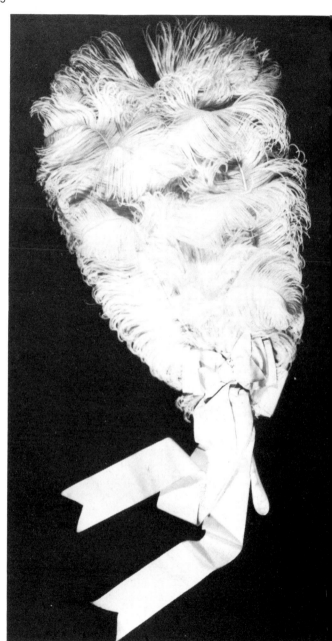

59 A feather fan, as advertised in Frederick Penberthy's catalogue; it is made of white ostrich plumes reminiscent of the Prince of Wales' feathers, with satin ribbon bows and ivory handle. An identical fan is illustrated in The Queen as one of the exhibits at the Fan-makers' exhibition held at Drapers' Hall on 16 May and presented by Mr. F. Penberthy. (23¾ in. — 715 mm. from the base of the handle to the top of the feathers.)

◁ 58 A photograph of an unknown lady in Dublin dressed for the ball, c. 1898. Her ostrich feather fan, with its loop and tassel, could have been a mail order from the London Glove Company or from a catalogue such as Penberthy's.

5

The Twentieth Century

By the late nineteenth century, the quality end of the fan trade was shared between a few well established houses. The history of the 'grandes maisons' of fans provides an insight into a business which reveals itself as quite a 'closed shop'. There was, too, a certain amount of intermarriage among the trade and the owners, which preserved a constant and loyal workforce, an army of well-tried suppliers, and consequently the goodwill of the customers. It is this which forms a link with the previous centuries, for it is thanks to the continuity of output and the way in which these intelligent tradespeople adapted to a changing world, that fans continued to be an accepted accessory well into the twentieth century.

A case in point is the Maison Duvelleroy, still in existence in 1983, the different owners of which had the good sense to preserve a name which had been a hallmark for quality fans since the 1830s. The London Duvelleroy, for example, was an independent and totally different establishment from the Paris Duvelleroy. Duvelleroy retail shops were strategically located in the most fashionable streets, their fans were also sold in the big department stores, and they were, to a degree, the intermediaries between the artists and the growing world of commerce embodied in haute couture and advertising, with which they were to become inextricably mixed.

This was the period often called 'Belle Epoque'; prevalent fashionable styles in all forms of art, and by implication in dress, were a revival of the modes and shapes of the end of the eighteenth century in France and the early nineteenth-century, Louis XVI, Directoire and Empire styles, with Art Nouveau for the younger more forward-looking, for the poets and less conservative members of society. Fans reflect these forms of art most accurately. Some of the ingenious small gauze fans embroidered all over with sequins were advertised by the fan-makers as the new 'Directoire' or 'Empire' fans. The larger ones with their gauze leaves often had insertions containing a painted scene with people in eighteenth-century-style costume. These styles were universally adopted in the West, in England in particular but, as always, with Paris setting the trend.

The London Duvelleroy evolved an exclusive design, made in France, but only sold in England, where the insertion was of transparent silk painted with a scene on one side and the reverse of the same scene on the other. For example, a 'pastiche' Louis XVI lady sits at a window conversing with a cupid whose head can be seen looking in at the window; on the reverse the lady's face appears in the window (from the outside of the building) and the little amorino's winged back is painted in. These vignettes are often of a Baroque shape, set within an embroidered border of sequins or even thin strips of translucent appliqué mother-of-pearl, with floral motifs in the reserves.

Most of the great fan-makers enlisted the services of the same painters and artists and catered for similar markets, so that, by the turn of the century, the same themes, whether of topographical, political or symbolic interest, were set for a season; thus it was that Duvelleroy, Kees and others would all, at the same time, be selling a poppy fan, for example, because haute couture had that season decreed it to be the flower in fashion. These crazes might be triggered off by a theatrical performance, a new poem, etc., and were treated in the style most relevant at the time. Fans were to a great extent a high fashion accessory until 1914 and the outbreak of the Great War.

It is fortunate that the French Duvelleroy archive is preserved in its entirety, the order-books confirming an impressive list of distinguished clients. At the turn of the century little gifts were reserved for Mr Duvelleroy's best customers in the shape of miniature fans, usually a much reduced copy of an eighteenth-century fan. These little fans have mistakenly been referred to as dolls' fans, or even minuet fans, and they are small enough for a doll, being 50 or 60 mm (2-2½ in.) long, but they were not made for that purpose. (Dolls' fans do exist, but they are of a cruder, much simpler quality, albeit of the same size.) At this time, fine fans were still one of the attributes of a lady, and

60a *A romantic fan from the London Duvelleroy (167 Regent Street). The blond tortoiseshell sticks and guards are ornamented with carved mother-of-pearl, the caramel-coloured gauze leaf is enhanced by a painted paper insertion in smoky tones, signed Faugeron, with rococo swirls outlined in tiny gold sequins. It comes in a brocaded box, satin lined, a corner of the interior lid stamped in gold letters: 'Manufactured in Paris'. c. 1895.*

60b *Clearly a small number of these exclusive fans were painted by the artist, as indicated by the notice in* The Queen, *p.1073, 7 December, 1895.*

THE LATEST FASHION IN FANS AT M. DUVELLEROY'S

61 Double image or two-way fans such as this mother-of-pearl and gauze creation, signed S. Drinot, were made in France exclusively for export, particularly to Britain. They were retailed by Duvelleroy in London. The Rococo-type scrollwork is outlined here with slivers of translucent mother-of-pearl, and underlined with tiny sequins. The whole conception and design are typical of the taste of the late 1890s and early 1900s. (6½ in. — 165 mm. long excluding the loop.)

62 A printed paper fan on wooden sticks, advertising the Chateau de Madrid restaurant in the Bois de Boulogne, Paris, designed by Paul Iribe, 1910-20.

little girls were taken to the pantomime before World War I in pretty frocks with sashes, wearing gloves and carrying a fan!

A particularly fashionable shape which had established itself before World War I was the arched fan, sometimes referred to as the 'fontange' or the 'palmette', in which the leaf is higher in the centre to the guard-sticks (fig. 62). It is a shape which adapted cunningly to the cut-out designs of the previous decade, and fitted well into the geometric patterns of emerging Art-Deco. This was a shape which found favour with Barbier and Iribe, both artists closely connected with fashion design and the stage; many other artists also realized its potential in advertising. Essentially a balloon shape, it had the advantage of constituting an ideal vehicle for the drawings of most modern artists, and by the '20s it is easy to indulge in

the exercise of juxtaposition, teaming the arched fan with the shape of the 'balloon' skirt.

Duvelleroy was the only French exhibitor of fans at the Turin International Exhibition of 1911. Having obtained the first gold medal ever awarded to fanmakers at the Exposition Universelle of 1889, there seems to have been no stopping him and the firm continued to carry off all the prizes at every other exhibition. The fans shown at Turin were a selection of the varied types and styles then in demand: a painted leaf by Maurice Leloir was mounted on sticks of blond tortoiseshell, the guards carved by Henneguy; there were a number of 'eventails de style' (pastiches of other periods) and novelties in lace, embroidery and feathers.

Statistics, together with a history of the fan, complete the report on Class 133D, costume accessories,

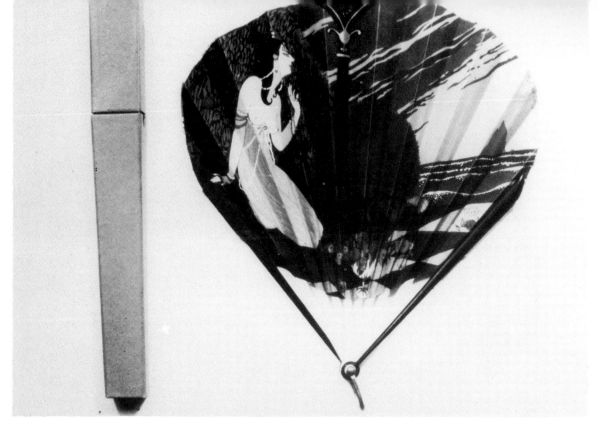

63, 64 *Printed for Paquin, in the strong colours inspired by Bakst and the Ballets Russes, a fan* designed by Paul Iribe, and another advertising fan by Barbier.

in the Turin Exhibition, and it is very evident that France was the leading country manufacturing fans for export all over the world, with Indo-China and Japan responsible for an active trade in the cheaper fan of the fixed type or the feather, paper or fabric fan on wooden sticks.

One of the many reports on the Milan International Exhibition five years earlier (1906) shows that this was indeed the case; from 1901 to 1905 exports of Italian fans, both of the finer and of the more ordinary types, had decreased, but imports of foreign fans, particularly those in the top price bracket from France, had risen in proportion. It is also noted that the Japanese pavilion included some 'delicious' fans.

Duvelleroy fans had achieved international repute, and George Duvelleroy in Paris employed a number of fashionable artists. Particularly favoured was Maurice Leloir, who painted fans given by the City of Paris to the Queen of Sweden and the Queen of Denmark.

Some private notes in George Duvelleroy's own hand dated 1929 are an invaluable source of information, for he mentions how the City of Paris, on several occasions, had commissioned him to provide fans which were destined to be a presentation gift to visiting consort sovereigns when they were received at the Hôtel de Ville. He describes the fan painted for the Empress of Russia by Louise Abbema, an artist with a flair for the fashions of the day. Her full length portrait of Mme George Duvelleroy, painted in 1905, (back cover) shows a dashing red-head in a wide-brimmed black hat, wearing a buttercup Empire-style gown, carrying one of the smaller spangled fans. She also designed a sign for La Maison Duvelleroy, and it was a printed copy of the fan she composed for the Russian state visit to Paris which was distributed at a soirée at the Opéra in honour of the Russian sailors (21 October 1893). Not surprisingly Mr Duvelleroy proudly boasts that 'we' (an almost royal plural) 'have made fans for the Queen of England, the Queen of Spain, the Queen of Roumania, the Princess of Monaco, the Princess of Orleans, etc., etc.'.

During and after World War I fans were increasingly relegated to the role of advertising — with the exception of court wear.

The War, with its terrible consequences, made even the most frivolous of women conscious of the disaster: prized fans and royal fans were sold in aid of the Red Cross and fans were designed and printed with patriotic messages to raise special funds, such as the one set up to help the emigré Russian soldiers.

If the Suffragettes in the earlier part of the century eschewed the use of the fan as too feminine a device,

there were still many who were ready and willing to make ample use of it in its increasingly varied shapes and sizes. One of the beauties of this era was Hazel Lavery, wife of the painter John Lavery, who retained the Edwardian style of dressing and was a close friend, in the War years, of Maud Cunard, mother of Nancy Cunard. Mrs Lavery favoured ostrich feathers, lace gloves and fans and wore orchids and clouds of tulle, as shown in the many portraits her husband painted of her. But new influences, particularly those of the famous Ballets Russes, were just around the corner.

Haute couture was perhaps at its most experimental in the first two decades of the century, and, more than ever before, the political and economic climates made advertising the 'in thing'. Hand-outs of fans became a habit with the great couturiers such as Paul Poiret, always seeking original new ideas and techniques, shapes and colours. When he opened his Maison Martine in 1911, there were typical 'Martine' fans with characteristic flower designs.

There was hardly a trade which, at some time or other, did not have an advertising fan but fans were not necessarily connected with haute couture, as were the great makes of perfume. There were advertising fans for trades from alcoholic beverages to underwear, with hotels and restaurants well up on the list of the many who made use of this effective mode of advertising. As late as the 1970s Thai Air lines had a small fan handout on their Far Eastern routes, and at least 1000 different varieties of advertising fans are known.

Vast quantities of very cheap Japanese fans were being imported, along with the other fancy goods which Japan was able to sell at cut prices to the West. Shops such as Liberty in London did much to promote the continued interest in fans from the East, retailing the better quality ones as well as the little Chinese and Japanese fans at one penny a dozen; these were placed in Christmas crackers.

The 'cotillon' fan, for dances or public balls, a cheaper version of the dress fan, was turned out in great numbers. Such fans were often given away as a souvenir at the fancy-dress ball which was a fixture on all the big liner routes, and they were in direct competition with the many Japanese imports which were also used for the same purpose. Sometimes they were stamped with the name of an advertising firm on the plain wooden guards.

It is useful to read women's magazines immediately after World War I, when already a change of attitude can be discerned. In 1919 (29 March) *The Queen* states that the fashionable 'girl' carries a fan regardless of the fact that 'such things' are more often confined

65 *A finely carved sandalwood Canton fan, complete with tassel, c. 1875. The colourful leaf is decorated in the traditional way with quantities of figures in applied silk robes with hands and faces of applied painted ivory. Complete with its purpose-made lacquer box, this type of fan was popular in Europe from the 1840s well into the twentieth century.*

◁ 66 *Half-plate autochrome study: the European girl wears a Chinese robe and holds a Canton fan and wears little fan-shaped ornaments in her hair. She is posed against an extraordinary hotch-potch including a Chinese vase with chrysanthemums — the traditional flower of Japan.*

67 *English court dress: The family of General Sir Robert Wigham, c. 1933, a photograph by Bassano. All the ladies wear the specified train, long gloves, fan and headgear.*

to the collectors' cabinet than brought into play in 'these days or nights! But then, no doubt she is dressed for the opera, not for the dance, and then beautiful fans come into their practical own again'. In November of that year there is a whole page devoted to the different types of fan to be seen either in the shops or in current use. There is a variation on the eagle wing fan of the previous century, now made from more prosaic goose feathers (fig. 51); one great ostrich plume used singly; a square fan of marabou feathers (the soft collar feathers of the vulture); an even greater ostrich feather fan with added strips which give it the name of 'waterfall'; a parchment leaf 'painted by Mr Ayres'; a fan of grey vulture feathers; the tail of a lyre-bird; peacock feathers and others. The writer of the article notes that Mr Jean Philippe Worth is: 'a great admirer of the fan, which is such an elegant attribute to women's charms', and it is true that he was one of the many couturiers to create fine plumage fans. He was also a patron of younger artists and ordered many fan designs from them.

Paquin, Lanvin, Doucet and Molyneux models of evening wear for 1919 are nearly all drawn or photographed with fans, with a predominance of feathers, which corresponds with the adornment of hats and headdress at this period.

Harrods, advertising their 'consummate Artistry Gifts for Christmas' (well in advance in early November 1919), offer ostrich feather fans mounted on three mother-of-pearl sticks in pink, yellow, mauve, emerald green, flame, white or black at £5 5s. 0d. or or six-inch black satin fans painted with various floral designs at 7s. 6d.

This was the era when pearl necklaces no longer simply encircled the neck, but fashion decreed they should fall down to the waist or lower still, then be twisted up in an original way. Soon girls would be floating about in short skirts with cigarette holders, twisting their long beads around a nervous manicured finger. The fan had no place in their lives, and was only for the debutante or elderly lady. It was in its court use that the fan now joined up with that other weapon, the sword, both accessories to dress, and both, by this time, purely ceremonial.

In his notes for 1929, Mr Duvelleroy states that: 'nowadays a lady may not be presented at the Courts of England and Spain without a fan; it was so for Court presentations in Germany. I do not know if this point of etiquette is current with other sovereigns, but is is very possible . . .'. Indeed, if one is to go by pictorial evidence, no court gown was complete without a complementary fan. In that twilight of royalty,

fans were *de rigueur* at court on all the more formal occasions until World War II (fig. 67).

In 1938, when the young King Farouk of Egypt married the beautiful Turkish Miss Zulfikar, a fan of pure white ostrich plumes, mounted on blonde tortoiseshell sticks, with diamond initials in the guards, was ordered from Duvelleroy in Paris, and Queen Farida is seen, in all the official photographs, holding not a bouquet but the majestic fan.

In July 1924, *Les Modes* showed three photographs of Duvelleroy fans, and still two of them are arched, shell-shaped, spangled, painted and trimmed with marabou; one is a lace fan. It is evident that the shapes and materials of the last century were still in use, together with man-made materials such as bakelite, celluloid and then plastic which were employed in an effort to replace more and more expensive and increasingly rare raw materials such as tortoiseshell and ivory for the sticks. The dearth of skilled artists in ivory carving in the West, and the ready availability of plastics of all kinds are largely responsible for the hideous fans sold in souvenir shops in the 1980s.

It is not hard to see how this vulgarization (in the same way that cheap printed fans at the end of the eighteenth century closed an epoch) lead in the end to an almost total demise of the fan. Not so easy to pinpoint is the reason why it no longer had a use as a fashion accessory, for, as has been seen, along with the finer and very expensive fans, there were less costly and indeed very cheap ones. The answer must lie in the revolutionary changes in the way of life of the western world after World War II. Unlike shoes, without which it is difficult to walk on hard pavements, or even gloves which are a necessity in a cold climate or dirty atmosphere, fans must claim to

68 *On 29 July 1981 Charles, Prince of Wales, heir* ▷ *to the throne of Great Britain, married Lady Diana Spencer. To commemorate the event, a talented silversmith T. Dobbie and his wife combined their skills to create a fan reminiscent of the first Elizabethan age. Three white ostrich feathers are fixed into a silver hallmarked handle; the Prince of Wales three feathers' crest in silver gilt decorates one side; and the reverse bears an inscription and date, and the logo of the Fan Circle International (a society created in 1975, through which the fan was sold). On the ball of the handle is the serial number of the limited edition of 25. The fan shown here is number 2. (Approximately 20 in. – 508 mm.)*

be a special-category fashion accessory. Jewellery satisfies a deep-rooted psychological need for adornment which fans may have done until new attitudes, new manners, indeed a totally new way of living, emerged. Where they are a necessity, fans are still used, but where no longer relevant in the practical and social order, they have become obsolete.

Signs of this phenomenon appeared when the big fan shops started to diversify: when Duvelleroy closed in Bond Street in the 1960s, the firm had been retailing silk blouses, scarves and evening bags as well as fans for over 30 years.

There is a curious parallel in the disappearance of that guardian of a lady's private life, the ladies' maid, and the simultaneous disappearance of fans and silk underwear, both coming under her specific care and attention. But it need not be surprising to observe young people in the 1980s sporting a fan from some distant part of the world as part of their 'gear'. However, during the heat wave of 1983 only two ladies were seen to be carrying fans at a royal garden party. The perverseness of fashion is such that the scorching summer of 1983 may have brought about a revival, for, tucked into the shoulder bags of all the Montana models for Spring 1984 is . . . a fan.

69 *A smart brisé ivory fan for evening wear, the guards entirely encrusted with turquoise and seed pearls, in its jewel-box leather case from Lambert, Jewellers, Coventry St, London. c. 1828.*

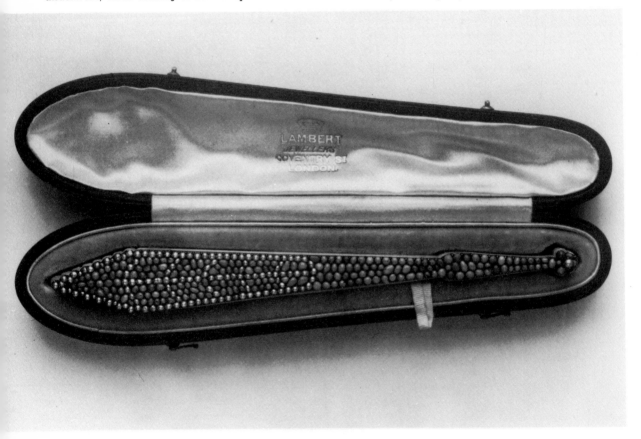

Appendix:
Fan Cases and Boxes

Mme Celnart, writing in the late 1820s, says in Chapter VIII of *L'Art de la Toilette* (a chapter incidentally entitled: ' . . . of the order of cleanliness which should preside over the exercises of dressing'): 'Fans should be folded neatly and put away in their boxes. The moment some part of these delicate instruments is seen to be unsound, you must immediately effect a repair. Sticking may be done with a quill dipped into egg white or a light solution of gum arabic.' At all times women prized their fans and regarded them as a treasured accessory which it was important to look after and preserve.

Fans were usually sold in boxes or cases, often bearing a label with the name of the shop or fan-maker — as early as the eighteenth century when the more usual case was made from pressed paper in the shape of a sheath to fit the fan neatly. The top could be pulled away quite easily, and the whole case was not unlike a cigar container. Tooled leather or shagreen boxes were specially made for the finer fans, and the fan fitted most snugly in its *own* box, with its characteristic hinges and hook clasps; but on these 'etuis' there is never a mention of the fan shop.

The little pressed paper boxes of the early nineteenth century were designed on the principle of the earlier ones, with the difference that they were smaller and squared, instead of rounded. On examination, the interiors sometimes reveal the printed paper lining, so that it is occasionally possible to attribute a country of origin if the label is missing.

The finer leather case continued in use for the more expensive fans, and some pretty fans reflecting the romantic tastes of the time with their 'gothic' pinnacles, had boxes into which they fit exactly and which resemble small coffins!

However elaborate their shape, in the nineteenth century fans had boxes of the appropriate shape and size, in an ever wider variety of materials; they were all proudly stamped with the maker's name and more often than not the town or country of purchase. The label on a cardboard box can sometimes give the location of the shop or shops. It is a fan box which reveals that Oskar Zeibig, Fächermacher, of 20 Struvestrasse, Dresden, exported fans to England, indeed to John C. B. Craddock of 489, Sauchiehall Street, Glasgow, in particular.

Fan boxes are relevant too in that the uniformity of the majority confirms the rarity and individuality of the fans contained in others. Oriental fans in boxes were solely for export, or for sale to Westerners. The many brisé lacquered fans, in their Chinese silk-covered boxes with little thong clasps, stamped 'Peking' or 'Canton', were patently for European consumption. The Canton 'Mandarin', or 'thousand face' fan, with its applied figures in silk robes, with ivory faces and hands, a model which was repeated in sizes corresponding to European fashions for nearly a century, came in a characteristic lacquer box lined on the inside of the lid with a colourful painting on silk and a small space cut out for those with tassels (fig. 65).

The great feather fans which seemed to herald the end of an era had their own large satin-covered boxes, fitted with special 'rests' for the sticks, and tapes to tie them in, in the manner of hat boxes. There is a basic difference and a quite clear distinction between these and the smaller fans, regarded more in the line of jewellery in their cases. Both were nevertheless fashion or dress accessories, designed to be worn.

Notes

INTRODUCTION

1 *The Archaeological Journal* CIII, 1946, figs 12, 14; and the *Bulletin of the Fan Circle International*, no. 20, pp. 28, 29.

2 Facher, *Realexikon zur Deutschen Kunstgeschichte*, p. 881, ill. 1.

3 B. Hughes, 'A Hoard of Elizabethan Jewellery', in *Country Life*, 4 February 1960.

4 R. Strong and Oman J. Trevelyan, *Elizabeth R*, 1971, p. 27.

5 Fan Circle and Debrett's Peerage, *Fans from the East*, 1978, p. 47.

6 Ibid.

7 Bertha de Vere Green, *Fans over the Ages*, 1975, p. 96.

CHAPTER 1

1 Fan Circle and Debrett's Peerage, *Fans from the East*, 1978, p. 47.

2 *Bulletin of the Fan Circle International*, no. 25, p. 23.

3 Levi Pisetzki, *Storia del Costume* III, 1964, pp. 105-6.

4 A Valabrègue, 'Les Eventails d'Abraham Bosse' in *Revue des Arts Décoratifs*, 1882, translated by H. Alexander in *Bulletin of the Fan Circle International*, no. 18, pp. 31-6.

5 F. Harcourt, ed., *Memoirs of the Verney Family*, Harvill Press, London.

6 Diana de Marly, 'Some aristocratic clothing accounts of the Restoration period in England' in *Waffen und Kostumkunde* no. 18, 1976, pp. 105-117.

7 Diana de Marly, 'Fashionable Suppliers 1660-1700' in *The Antiquaries' Journal*, pp. 334-47.

8 Ibid.

9 Samuel Pepys, *Diaries*, edited by R.C. Latham and W. Mathews, Bell and Sons, 11 vols., 1970-1982, pp. 142 and 156.

10 Diana de Marly, 'Fashionable Suppliers . . .' op. cit.

11 *Lettres, Statuts et Arrest de la Cour de Parlement confirmatif d'icelles, accordées en faveur des Maistres Eventaillistes; et Compositeurs d'Eventails, de la Ville, Fauxbourgs & Banlieue de Paris* MDC LXX1X. Extrait des Registres du Conseil d'Estat Aij, Aiij, etc., pp. 1-16.

12 'Paris du Règne d'Henri II à la Régence', in *Bulletin du Musée Carnavalet*, nos. 1, 2, 1970, p. 29.

CHAPTER 2

1 Bernard Ross-Collins, *A Short Account of the Worshipful Company of Fan-Makers*, 1950.

2 See *Stamp Book of Admittances*, 1747; Records of the Worshipful Company of Fan-Makers; earlier records have been destroyed.

3 N. Irons, *Fans of Imperial China*, 1981, pp. 14, 18.

4 H. Alexander, 'Some Facets of Fan Collecting', in *Antique Collecting*, vol. 14, no. 7, 1979, pp. 8, 11.

5 Dr I. Van Eeghen, 'De Amsterdamse Waaierindustrie in de 18de eeuw'.

6 S. Mayor, *Collecting Fans*, 1980, p. 10.

7 Savary des Brouslons, *Dictionnaire Universel de Commerce*, vol. 1 A to E, 1723, pp. 1178-9.

8 S. Blondel, *Histoire des éventails chez tous les peuples et à toutes les époques*, 1875.

9 *Fans and the Grand Tour*, catalogue of exhibition at the Brighton Museum, 1982.

10 Ibid.

11 Ibid.

12 Levi Pisetzki, op. cit.

13 Hammar, 'Solfjadar fran 1700 Valet' in *Kulturen*, 1976, pp. 97-116, Lund, Sweden.

14 Fan Circle and Debrett's Peerage, *Fans from the East*, 1978, p. 52.

15 V. Philippe, 'Un eventail peint par Marie Antoinette', in *Connaissance des Arts*, 1963, no. 141.

16 Bachaumont, *Memoires Secrets*.

17 D. George, *Catalogue of Political and Personal Satires in the British Museum*.

18 M. Vautel, 'Charolotte Corday'. Deposition of the witness Citizen Laurent Bas; he declares that on Saturday 13 July 1793, a woman whose appearance he describes in detail, and who was holding a fan, asked to speak to the Citizen Marat.

19 Towle, *The Young Gentleman and Lady's Private Tutor*, 1771.

20 L'A de Caraccioli, *Le Livre de Quatre Couleurs*, Paris, 1760.

21 Lady Charlotte Schreiber, *Fans and Fan Leaves*.

22 E. Oldham, 'The Fan, A Gentleman's Accessory', in *The Connoisseur*, no. 125, pp. 14-20.

CHAPTER 3

1 M.F. Bordez, 'La fabrication des montures d' Eventail à Sainte Geneviève (Oise)', in *Bulletin du Comité des travaux historiques et scientifiques*, 1904.

2 B. de Vere Green, op. cit., p. 277.

3 *Dictionnaire Petit Larousse Illustré*, 1945, pp. 785, 815.

4 *Paris Fans of the Belle Epoque*, catalogue of exhibition in Bristol, 1983.

5 H Bouchot, 'L'Histoire par les Eventails populaires', in *Les Lettres et les Arts* (Paris, January and July 1883); and according to G. Wooliscroft Rhead fans were found at Vanier in the Rue Caumartin.

6 H. Bouchot, 'Le Luxe Français — La Restauration', 1893, (Quadrille de Marie Stuart, 2 March, 1829, etc).

CHAPTER 4

1 M.F. Bordez, op. cit.

2 Ibid.

3 *Eventaillistes*, in Paris exhibition reports for 1867, p. 5 *Découpure ou grillage mécanique dû à l'invention d'Alphonse Baud*, 1859.

4 D. Didron, *Rapport su les Arts Décoratifs à l'Exposition*, 1878.

5 K. Staniland and S.M. Levey, 'Queen Victoria's Wedding Dress and Lace, in *Costume*, no. 17, 1983.

6 L. Valentine, *The Queen, her early life and reign*, 1887, p. 331.

7 *The Queen (the Lady's Newspaper)*, 17 December, 1887, p. 824.

8 E. Lefèvre, *Le Commerce et l'Industrie de la Plume pour Parure*, 1914.

9 Ibid.

10 *The Queen*, 29 April, 1876, p. 290.

11 D. Holman-Hunt, *My Grandfather, his Wives and Loves*, 1969, p. 261.

12 Fan Circle and Debrett's Peerage, *Fans from East*, p. 55.

13 M. Rosenberg, *Alte und Neue Fächer aus der Wettbewerbung und Ausstellung zu Karlsruhe*, 1891, p. 15.

14 B. Kendell, 'Concerning Fans', in *The Connoisseur*, 1903, vol. VII pp. 14-20.

Glossary

Arched See *Fontange*.

Bakelite a synthetic resin used for some twentieth-century fan sticks and guards.

Brisé a fan consisting of sticks only forming a flat surface when open, held together at the top by a cord or ribbon, threaded, slotted or stuck on.

Canons a form of wide breeches worn in the seventeenth century.

Celluloid a solid, hard, transparent substance made from a mixture of camphor and cellulose nitrate, an early plastic, highly flammable.

Circular See *Cockade*.

Cloisonné a form of enamel work, usually made in the Orient, in which the designs are supported by vertical partitions which help to retain the vitreous substance.

Cockade (fan) either of the brisé or pleated kind which opens up *around* the pivot set at the centre of the fan (as opposed to being at its base). The fan is therefore circular or semi-circular in shape — sometimes called *parasol fan* or *circular*.

Fontange (fan) a name given to the type of fan in which the guard sticks are shorter than the leaf at its apex — known also as *palmette* and *arched*.

Gorge the part of the fan immediately above the pivot end.

Guard (sticks) the two outer sticks of a fan, usually stouter and more highly decorated.

Leaf See *Mount*.

Loop usually a curved attachment to the bottom end of a fan, held in place by the rivet, whereby a fan may be suspended from a cord or ribbon.

Mica a silico-aluminate of potassium, iron or magnesium, presenting the aspect of a scaly, bright stone. The scales form blades of shiny, transparent substance used for the adornment of some fans.

Mould (fan) also referred to as a *press:* two identical sheets of pleated stout paper, sometimes joined at one end, quadrangular-shaped. The fan leaf is inserted between the two sheets, folded up, and the whole inserted into a tight sheath where it is left for some time in a warm atmosphere. On removal from the mould the fan is impressed with permanent pleating.

Mount (fan) the portion of the fan which is placed onto and over the ribs. It is also known as the *leaf;* it can be pleated and made from a variety of materials such as paper, vellum, silk, cotton etc. It may be single or double.

Paper (fan) the unmounted leaf of a fan; a term used in the seventeenth and eighteenth centuries.

Palmette See *Fontange*.

Parasol (fan) See *Cockade*.

Piqué a form of decoration mainly on tortoiseshell and ivory, developed in Italy, consisting of decorative shapes made by dots of precious metal (gold or silver) set into the host material.

Pivot consisting of a small metal rod inserted through the lower part of the sticks of the fan and around which the fan can revolve. It is terminated at either end by a 'stop' which holds it in place and prevents slipping. These 'stops' are sometimes referred to as pivot end or *rivet* and are sometimes made of paste; in special cases they can be small jewelled buttons.

Press See *Mould*.

Reserves the outer sides of the leaf of a fan.

Reverse the back of the leaf, usually the side facing the wearer.

Ribs the upper part of the sticks which support the leaf.

Rivet the 'stops' on either side of the pivot. See *Pivot*.

Sticks the principal part of the fan, the skeleton, as it were, which also contains the articulation.

Vellum calf skin specially treated and prepared to form a paper-like substance, used for early fan leaves.

Vernis Martin a varnish invented by the Martin family (*c.* 1720 – 1758). "Vernis Martin" fans are usually of the brisé kind and so-called because their painted, varnished surface appears to resemble known work from the Martin workshops.

Museums to Visit

Mrs Mary Rhoads has compiled a guide to the Fan Collection of American Museums and Historical Societies — obtainable from:

PO Box 763
Kennett Square 1
P.A. 19348
USA

(*Fan Circle International Bulletin*, no. 24, p. 17, Summer 1983.)

I have therefore given here a list of museums, etc., in Great Britain and on the Continent of Europe, which is intended only as a preliminary compilation.

GREAT BRITAIN

London
Victoria & Albert Museum
The British Museum (Dept of Prints & Drawings, Schreiber Collection)
The Museum of London
Horniman Museum (Ethnographic)
Museum of Mankind (Ethnographic)

Outside London
Waddesdon Manor, Nr. Aylesbury
Museum of Costume, Bath
City Museum & Art Gallery, Birmingham
Art Gallery & Museums, Brighton
Museum & Art Gallery, Bristol
Fitzwilliam Museum, Cambridge
Amgueddfa Werin Cymru, St Fagans, Cardiff
National Museum of Antiquities, Edinburgh
Royal Scottish Museum, Edinburgh
Royal Albert Memorial Museum, Exeter
Glasgow Museum & Art Gallery, Glasgow
Burrell Collection, Glasgow
Temple Newsam House, Leeds
Luton Museum, Luton
Gallery of English Costume, Manchester
Laing Art Gallery & Museum, Newcastle

Ashmolean Museum, Oxford (Oriental)
Pitt Rivers Museum, Oxford (Ethnographic)
Harris Museum & Art Gallery, Preston
Reading Museum & Art Gallery, Reading
The Worthing Museum, Sussex

AUSTRIA
Museum für Völkerkunde, Vienna (Ethnographic)
Osterreichisches Museum für angewandte Kunst
    (Figdor Collection), Vienna

BELGIUM
Musées Royaux d'Art et d'Histoire, Brussels

FRANCE
Musée de l'Arletan, Arles
Musée des Arts Décoratifs, Bordeaux
Musée de la Soie, Lyon
Musée du Textile, Lyon
Musée Lyonnais des Arts Décoratifs, Lyon
Musée Carnavalet, Paris
Musée de l'Hotel de Cluny, Paris
Musée de la Mode et du Costume, Paris
Musée des Arts Décoratifs, Paris
Musée du Prieuré St Germain-en-Laye

GERMANY
Museum für Volkerkunde, Berlin (Ethnographic)
Museum für Kunsthandwerk, Frankfurt
Museum für Kunst und Gewerbe, Hamburg
Atoner Museum, Hamburg
Germanisches Nationalmuseum, Nuremberg

ITALY
Museo Stibbert, Florence
Castello Sforcesco, Milan
Museo Poldi Pozzoli, Milan
National Museum, Naples
Museo di Arte Orientale, Rome
Museo di Palazzo Venezia, Rome
Museo Correr, Venice

NETHERLANDS
Rijksmuseum, Amsterdam
Netherlands Kostuummuseum, The Hague
Museum Boyans van Benningen, Rotterdam

PORTUGAL
Museu Nacional dos Coches, Lisbon

SPAIN
Museo de Indumentara (Colecion Rocamora),
   Barcelona
Museo Cambô, Barcelona
Palacio Fernân Nuñez, Madrid
Palacio Real di Aranjuez, nr. Madrid

SWEDEN
National Museum, Stockholm

SWITZERLAND
Kirschgarten Museum, Basel
Historisches Museum, Basel
Musée d'Art et d'Histoire, Geneva
Chateau de Nyon, Nyon
Schweizerisches Landemuseum, Zurich

Bibliography

Adburgham, A., *A Punch History of Manners & Modes, 1841-1940*, Hutchinson, London, 1961

Allemagne, H.R., *Les Accessoires du Costume et du Mobilier*, Schomit., Paris, 1928

Armstrong, N., *A Collector's History of Fans*, Studio Vista, London & New York, 1974

Armstrong, N., *The Book of Fans*, Colour Library International, 1978

Aubrey, J., *Aubrey's Brief Lives* (edited by Oliver Lawson Dick), Secker & Warburg, London, 1949

Bachaumont, L.P. de, *Memoires secrets pour servir à l'histoire de la République des Lettres en France*, J. Adamson, London, 1783-89

Baines, B., *Fashion Revivals*, Batsford, London, 1981

Barò Escalante, C.M., *Eventails anciens*, Payot, Lausanne, 1957

Bennett, A.G., and Berson, R., *Fans in Fashion*, catalogue of an Exhibition at the Fine Arts Museum, San Francisco, 1981

Blanc, C., *Art in Ornaments and Dress*, Chapman & Hall 1877, translated from the French, *L'Art dans la parure et dans le vêtement*, Renovard, Paris, 1875

Blondel, S., *Histoire des éventails chez tous les peuples et à toutes les époques*, L. Renovard, Paris, 1875

Blum, A., *Costume of the Western World. The Last of the Valois and Early Bourbon*, edited by James Laver, G.G. Harrap & Co. 1951

Blum, S., *Victorian Fashions & Costumes from Harpers Bazaar*, Dover Publications, New York, 1974

Bordez, M.F., 'La Fabrication des Montures d'Eventails etc', in *Bulletin du Comité des traveaux historiques etc*, Paris, 1904.

Bouchot, H., *Le Luxe Français*, La Restauration-Librairie Illustrée, Paris, 1893

Brantôme P. de Bourdille, Seigneur de, *Vie des Dames Illustres françaises et étrangères*, ed. Louis Moland, Paris, 1922

Brouslons, J. Savary des, *Dictionnaire Universel de Commerce*, Paris, 1723

Buck, A.M. *Victorian Costume and Costume Accessories*, H. Jenkins, London, 1961

Buissot, E., *Collection d'éventails anciens des XVII et XVIII Siècles*, Paris, 1890

Bulletin of the Fan Circle International, 1975 onwards

Burney, F., *The Journals & Letters* (10 Vols), ed. J. Hemlow, Oxford University Press, 1972-1982

Byrde, P., *A Frivolous Distinction*, Bath City Council, 1979

Catalani, C., *Waaiers*, Bussum, Holland, 1973

Cust, L., *The Catalogue of the Collection of Fans and Fan Leaves presented to the Trustees of the British Museum by Lady Charlotte Schreiber*, 1893

Diderot, D. et d'Alembert, *Encyclopédie*, Paris, 1765

Falluel, F., and the Fan Circle International, *Paris Fans of the Belle Epoque*, catalogue of an exhibition at Bristol 1983

Fans from the East, Debrett's Peerage Ltd., for the Birmingham City Museum & Art Gallery, the Victoria & Albert Museum and the Fan Circle, London 1978

Fraipont, G., *L'Art de Composer et de peindre l'eventail l'écran, le paravent*, H. Laurens, Paris, 1896

Franklin, A., *La Vie Privée d'Autrefois et notice des Emaux*, Plon, Paris, 1887-1901

Ginsburg M., *An Introduction to Fashion Illustration*, Victoria & Albert Museum/Compton Press/Pitman, London, 1980

Ginsburg, M., *Victorian Dress in Photographs*, Batsford, London, 1982

Gostelow, M., *The Fan*, Gill & Macmillan, Dublin, 1976

Hammar, B., 'Fans in the 18th Century', in *Kulturen*, Lund, Sweden, 1976

Irons, N., *Fans of Imperial China*, Kaiserreich Kunst,

Hong Kong, 1981

Jong, M.C. de, *Waaiers & Mode 18ᵉ eeuw tot Heden*, Catalogue of Exhibition Nederlands Kostummuseum, 1979

Laver, J., *Taste and Fashion*, G.G. Harrap and Co, London, 1937

Leary, E., *Fans in Fashion*, catalogue of an exhibition at Temple Newsam Leeds & Platt Hall, Manchester, 1975

Lefèvre, E., *Le Commerce et l'Industrie de la Plume pour Parure*, Paris, 1914,

Leloir, M., *L'Histoire du Costume de l'Antiquité à 1914*, H. Erust, Paris, 1938

Levi-Pisetzki, *Storia del Costume*, Instituto Editoriale Italiano, Milan, 5 vols, 1964

Martène, E., and Durard, U., eds., *Chronicles of Tours*, Paris, 1724-33

Mayor, S., *Collecting Fans*, Studio Vista, London, 1980

Morse, H.B., *The Chronicles of the East India Company Trading to China 1635-1834*, Clarendon Press, Oxford 1926

Ohm, A., *In Reallexikon zur Deutschen Kunstgeschichte*, Stuttgart, 1972

Percival Maciver, *The Fan Book*, T. Fisher & Unwin, London, 1920

Petit, E., *Le Passé, le Présent et l'Avenir, Etudes sur la Fabrication de l'Eventail*, Versailles, 1895

Planché, J.R., *A cyclopaedia of Costume; or Dictionary of Dress*, 2 vols, London 1876-79

Planché, J.R., *Souvenir of the Bal Costumé given by Queen Victoria at Buckingham Palace, 12 May 1842*, London, 1843

Redgrave, S., *Catalogue of the Loan Exhibition of Fans at South Kensington*, London, 1870

Rhead, G. Wooliscroft, *History of the Fan*, Kegan Paul, London, 1910

Rosenberg, M., *Alte und Neue Fächer aus der Wettbewerbung und Ausstellung zu Karlsruhe*, Gulack & Schnak, 1891

Ross-Collins, B., *A Short Account of the Worshipful Company of Fan-Makers*, London, 1950

Schreiber, Lady Charlotte, *Fans and Fan Leaves*, J. Murray, London, 1880-90

Sociedad Española de Amigos del Arte, *Exposicion de El Abanico en Espagña*, Blas, Madrid 1920

Strong, R., and Trevelyan, Oman J., *Elizabeth R.*, Secker, London, 1971

Strong, R., *The English Icon*, Paul Mellon Foundation, 1969

Strong, R., *Tudor and Jacobean Portraits*, H.M.S.O., London, 1969

Tal, F., *De Waaier Colletie Felix Tal*, catalogue of exhibition, Utrecht, 1967

Tour du Pin, Mme de la, H.L., *Memoirs*, edited by F. Harcourt, Harvill Press, London, 1969

Uzanne, O., *l'Eventail*, A Quantin, Paris 1882, English translation: *The Fan*, Nimmo & Barn, London, 1884

Valentine, L., *The Queen, Her Early Life & Reign*, F. Warne & Co, 1887

Vecellio, C., *Habiti Antichi & Moderni*, Sessa, Venice, 1598

Vere-Green, de., B., *A Collector's Guide to Fans over the Ages*, F. Muller, London, 1975

Verney, F.P., *Memoirs of the Verney family during the Seventeenth Century*, 2 vols, Longman, 1904

Verney, F.P., *Memoirs of the Verney family during the Civil War*, 4 vols, Longman, 1892-99

Walker, R., *Catalogue of the Cabinet of Old Fans*, Sotheby, Wilkinson & Hoge, 1882

Waugh, N., *The Cut of Women's Clothes 1600-1930*, Faber and Faber, 1968

White, Palmer, *Poiret*, Studio Vista, London, 1973

Wildeblood, J., and Brinson, P., *The Polite World*. Oxford University Press, 1965

Zauber des Fächers, *Fächer aus dem Besitz des Museum*, Altonauer Museum, Hamburg, 1974

Index